P9-DBT-392

The
Ethos
of the Bible

The Ethos of the Bible

BIRGER GERHARDSSON

Translated by Stephen Westerholm

FORTRESS PRESS   PHILADELPHIA

This book is a translation of *"med hela ditt hjärta."* *Om Bibelns ethos,*
copyright © 1979 by LiberLäromedel, Lund.

Biblical quotations from the Revised Standard Version of the Bible,
copyrighted 1946, 1952, © 1971, 1973 by the Division of Christian Education of the National Council of the Churches of Christ in the U.S.A.,
are used by permission.

Biblical quotations from *The New English Bible,* © The Delegates of
the Oxford University Press and The Syndics of the Cambridge University Press 1961, 1970, are reprinted by permission.

COPYRIGHT © 1981 BY FORTRESS PRESS

All rights reserved. No part of this publication may be reproduced,
stored in a retrieval system, or transmitted in any form or by any means,
electronic, mechanical, photocopying, recording, or otherwise, without
the prior permission of the copyright owner.

Library of Congress Cataloging in Publication Data

Gerhardsson, Birger.
The ethos of the Bible.

Translation of: "Med hela ditt hjärta."
Bibliography: p.
Includes index.
1. Ethics in the Bible.   I. Title.
BS680.E84G4713   220.6   81–43077
ISBN 0–8006–1612–X   AACR2

9013D81   Printed in the United States of America   1–1612

Contents

CONTENTS

Preface

This presentation of the ethos of the Bible was originally written for an interdisciplinary collection of studies dealing with ethics and Christian faith and published in Swedish by Gustaf Wingren (*Etik och kristen tro* [Lund: LiberLäromedel, 1971]). I have since revised and extended my own contribution and published it as a separate book under the Swedish title *"med hela ditt hjärta." Om Bibelns ethos* (Lund: LiberLäromedel, 1979). It is this latter version which has here been translated.

When my study was written for the symposium volume, there was no need to comment on the fact that with but a few, deliberate exceptions, I keep quite strictly to biblical times. Theologians from other disciplines carried the discussion further historically and *ideengeschichtlich*, analyzed problems systematically, and introduced factors which must be heeded when one attempts to shed light on ethical issues today. Now, when my contribution is published separately, I ought perhaps to point out that my largely historical discussion needs of course to be supplemented from a systematic point of view and with attention to the particular conditions of our time and of the society in which we live. Cooperation between the theological disciplines is essential. In order to facilitate such cooperation, specialists will have to venture a *short* distance beyond the strict boundaries of their disciplines. I have attempted to keep this in mind in my presentation of the material.

The Swedish title of the book (*med hela ditt hjärta*—"With Your Whole Heart") is of course taken from the fundamental command in the Bible of the Christian church, Deut. 6:4–5. Distinctive to this presentation are the attempts made to show the role this command played—not only through the profound idea at its root, but also through its very *wording*—for many of those who speak in the ancient texts revealing the Bible's ethos.

PREFACE

Unless otherwise noted, Scripture quotations are translated according to my rendering of the original.

I thank my friend Stephen Westerholm for his careful, reliable translation work.

Lund, 1980   BIRGER GERHARDSSON

Introduction

The Bible of the Christian church contains sixty-six books; together they make up a mosaic whose diversity is much more apparent than its unity and basic patterns. To present the Bible's ethos in a satisfactory way within the scope of a hundred pages or so is an almost impossible task. The situation, however, is hardly unique: all our knowledge is necessarily fragmentary, and we find ourselves continually faced with more or less "impossible" tasks.

No individual book in the Bible—much less the Bible as a whole— was written in order to present a carefully devised moral philosophy or system of ethics. This fact has led certain exegetes to conclude that there is no adequate base for writing a "biblical ethics." Can such a book be written? The answer to that question depends on what is meant by "ethics" and the way in which one intends to handle the material. Obviously, much in the Bible *does* deal with the kind of people we ought to be and the way we ought to behave; that is, with humankind's "ethos" in the sense of attitudes and behavior which conform to norms. This is naturally something which can be described. The first task is then that of analyzing each book or group of books by itself. That being done, it ought not to be impossible to point out those essential characteristics which make up the basic *unity* in the midst of the Bible's *diversity*, thus providing a synthetic sketch of the Bible's ethos. That there nonetheless are many pitfalls along the way is self-evident.

In this comparatively brief account, I have chosen to present the material in the following way. In the final chapter I attempt to provide a summary picture and characterization of the *Bible's* ethos. The main part of the book, however, is made up of an historical description of the ethos of (1) postexilic Judaism and (2) early Christianity against the background of the general conditions under

1

which the people involved were living and the whole of their outlook on life (their faith, view of life, ideals). The period with which we are largely concerned is that stretching from about five hundred years before Christ to the mid–second century A.D.

Limitations of space have necessitated a good deal of simplification, and I have had to choose those areas and aspects which seem to me to be of special importance. Particularly regrettable is the fact that justice cannot be done to the Old Testament material. Its breadth and diversity—both in character and content—are far from adequately treated here. To cite but one example, the wisdom literature could be dealt with at length. In my presentation, the Old Testament material has had to serve primarily—if not solely—either as background or as a base for that of the New. My procedure is motivated by the conviction that fundamental Old Testament norms come to expression even in an account of early Christianity's ethos. The young church regarded its teaching as the adequate exposition, in the age of fulfillment, of what is written in "the law and the prophets." The exclusive aspect of this claim can of course be debated; but there is no denying the astonishing extent to which early Christianity actually did draw from the well of the Old Testament Scriptures.

With regard to the presentation of the New Testament, I have chosen not to give what would necessarily have been a very superficial survey of the whole area covered by the twenty-seven books. Instead, I have given three representatives of early Christianity comparatively detailed treatment. Naturally, the attempt was made to keep *all* the books of the Bible in mind in writing the synthetic chapter with which this study concludes (chapter six).

The three representatives of early Christianity chosen are Matthew, Paul, and John. In one respect, the first of these stands in a class by himself. None of the other "authors" of the Bible concerns himself with ethics in so conscious and consistent a way as Matthew. Paul does not show the same interest in the task of working out a unified ethical outlook. Nonetheless, out of his intensive wrestlings with the fundamental problems of human existence, a fairly consistent total view does emerge. Within it we find an abundance of ethical material which bears the marks of profound personal involvement and an urgent sense of the need for clarity.

Moreover, Matthew and Paul are of special interest in that both have deliberately reflected on the difference between the ethos with which they once conformed and the one they now embrace, "in Christ." Both have left the "ethos of the Jewish theocracy" behind them, but they have clearly indicated, for their own sake and for those holding fast to the principles they once maintained, what motivated the change. Nor is their argumentation of a kind that their earlier colleagues could easily dismiss.

My third choice for a representative of early Christianity has fallen on John. Admittedly, there is within the Johannine writings remarkably little which deals in a *concrete* way with ethical problems. Still, this group of writings is an important and conspicuous segment of the New Testament, and as part of the profound total outlook we encounter in them, the ethical dimension does find a place. Moreover, its treatment is a radical one, determined by principles which are quite clearly enunciated. The markedly *theological* ethics of the Johannine writings thus deserve a place even within the limitations of our study.

Arguments could be raised for treating these three in different sequences. I have chosen to discuss Matthew first since he is the one most closely tied to the concrete material from and about the one who is the starting point and focus for them all—Jesus himself. Paul writes, to be sure, before Matthew does, but the letter form he uses is freer and permits treating the questions with a greater distance. The same consideration makes it reasonable to treat John last. Here the distance is still greater; the problems have been reduced to a few decisive questions in a manner betraying both simplification and depth.

I assume that the reader has some elementary acquaintance with matters discussed in New Testament introductions. Here I would only point out that I speak of Matthew, Paul, and John, using the *conventional* names for those who have given us the First Gospel, the Pauline corpus of Epistles, and John's Gospel and First Epistle respectively. Thus I do not treat distinctly the various strata of Matthew's Gospel, in spite of the fact that I do not believe the final redactor was the same person as the scribally trained man whose influence dominated the Matthean circle. I take, in other words, the First Gospel in the form in which we find it in the critically established Greek text. In the chapter dealing with the Pauline corpus, I do not exclude the "deutero-Pauline" Epistles, in spite of the fact that I share the doubts of many whether Paul himself composed the pastorals; this doubtfulness extends—though not in the same degree—to Ephesians and Colossians. (I have not, however, been convinced by the arguments raised against Pauline authorship of 2 Thessalonians.) Naturally I do place the main emphasis on the oldest and undisputed Pauline Letters. In the chapter dealing with the Johannine material as well, I take the writings as we have them without distinguishing strata. Primarily I am concerned with the Gospel and First Epistle, the writings of greatest importance for our purposes. I do not, however, leave the other three books entirely out of the picture.

In order to give readers the opportunity to confirm what is said and to investigate the questions on their own, I have quoted quite a number of important biblical texts and listed numerous biblical references in the course of the presentation. Still, it has of course been necessary to limit the number given. Hence the references are by no means exhaustive.

I do not discuss in this book the problems arising from the fact that the biblical writings are by nature patriarchal and male-dominated (androcentric). Nor do I pay special attention to this matter in my account of biblical attitudes and outlooks. The whole problem is extremely complicated; male dominance has even left profound marks on the language itself.

That I have so little to say about the socioeconomic background of biblical attitudes is not because of a lack of interest. The task of clarifying this side of the problems we discuss is virtually an impossible one. Biblical concepts and patterns of thought have come from many corners; they have, as authoritative tradition, passed through many types of society and been used by teachers with a variety of economic and social backgrounds before the texts were recorded. To a certain extent this is even true of the New Testament material. Those who had influence within early Christianity were molded by upbringings in a number of different milieus and classes of society, and it certainly took time before fairly uniform ways of thinking prevailed within the congregations—in spite of all the attempts made in this direction.

BIBLIOGRAPHICAL NOTE

With regard to problems of methodology, see most recently the concise but instructive article by G. Strecker, "Strukturen einer neutestamentlichen Ethik," in *Zeitschrift für Theologie und Kirche* 75 (1978): 117–46 (with references to other literature). See also the bibliography at the close of this book.

1

Attitudes Toward History and Politics

THE LACK OF POLITICAL FREEDOM

During the period stretching from the Babylonian exile until the close of the New Testament era, the Jewish people in Palestine were subject almost continuously to the rule of one of the great powers: Persian, Egyptian, Syrian, and Roman. To be sure, the foreign yokes varied in kind and severity. Nor did all groups and classes of Jews find them equally burdensome. Here, however, by way of introduction, we overlook qualifying details like these in order to stress a factor of some significance for an understanding of the ethos both of postexilic Judaism and of Christianity in its earliest stages. A people subject to a foreign power has a limited scope of activity: bold, creative, enterprising endeavors are hampered. In the postexilic period, Jews were condemned to passivity in the most important forums of politics. Active impulses had to be channeled into areas regarded as permissible.

Naturally, a yearning for freedom and some smoldering opposition did exist. National sovereignty was regarded by most Jews as desirable. Dreams of freedom found stimulation in the native heritage kept alive from older, freer times when even peaceable folk acknowledged that there was "a time for war," that battle might be necessary and holy. Many depictions of "Yahweh's wars" against the enemies and oppressors of his people are contained in the books of the Old Testament. In the Scriptures, enthusiastic accounts of battle could be found. There too were inspiring portrayals of leaders bold and irrepressible, whom God raised up to be "saviors" (liberators), and who thus advanced victoriously at the head of the

7

armies of Israel (for example, Judges 3—8, 11—12, 13—16). There could be found as well prophetic announcements of a marvelous man of God who one day would break "the yoke of his burden, and the staff for his shoulder, the rod of his oppressor . . . as on the day of Midian" (Isa. 9:4 RSV). Texts and examples like these could easily be brought to life when the need arose to inspire bands of armed men to revolt in the struggle for liberation (see, for example, 2 Macc. 8:23; 15:7–10).

In fact, there were occasions when—at least for a limited period and in a limited area—some such liberator did succeed in throwing aside the foreign yoke and achieving independence. The longest-lasting period of freedom was that brought about by the Maccabees (142–63 B.C.). It is typical that both Judas Maccabeus and his brother Simon are portrayed in messianic terms in the books devoted to their accomplishments; the heroic poems in 1 Macc. 3:3–9 and 14:6–15 are not the only examples of this. The Romans, however, took control in 63 B.C. and put an end to Jewish independence. The Herodian vassal rulers were regarded by Jews neither as legitimate nor as representatives of their people. Time and again in the period which followed, some messianic, liberating figure arose and gathered bands for revolt and rebellion. But the superior forces of the Romans quickly restored order, ruthlessly drowning the disturbances in blood. The freedom fighters met with their greatest success during the revolts of A.D. 66–70 and 132–35, winning to their cause even pious people known for their love of peace. The rebel leader Bar Kochba was believed to be Messiah even by the great rabbi Akiba. But the superiority of Roman might was too great. Not even the most fiery fanaticism and exceptional bravery could keep the Jews from being conquered and mercilessly subjugated in the end.

The centuries of foreign rule accustomed the Jews to showing patience and biding their time. The full freedom for which they dreamed was awaited as a gift from God. In its time—sooner or later—it would come, either as the result of a holy war waged at the right moment by God's people, or as the result of a miraculous intervention by Messiah or by God himself in solitary majesty. Hopes for the future took varying forms. At one extreme we find views marked by the fury of fanaticism and the lust for bloody revenge; at the other, an intensive but sober hope for a coming *judgment*, when justice at last will be done, and both the good and the evil will be treated according to their deserts.

In the meantime, the lesson of accepting the lack of political freedom had to be learned. The Jewish historian Josephus tells of the rebel Judas from Gamala (in Galilee), who repudiated Roman rule: in his view, God alone is to be acknowledged as Lord; no mortal may be given that title (*War* 2.8.1; *Ant.* 18.1.6). This outlook, however, was not the normal one. Most Jews during the centuries immediately before and after the beginning of our era believed that the "people of God" need a human "shepherd," and that they can fulfill their mission and "walk worthy of their calling" even when God sees fit to chasten them with a foreign (human) yoke.

In early Christian documents we meet the occasional passage expressing vindictiveness and the desire for revenge (for example, Rev. 19:11–21), but such passages are remarkably few and incidental. The principles governing Christian views are quite different, as the sources show us with a striking unanimity. Certain scholars have attempted to demonstrate that Jesus of Nazareth was in fact a liberator with a program for political and social revolution, but it requires an unusual amount of violence to the sources to extract from them support for such a view.

It is clear enough that the impact of Jesus' ministry aroused current messianic expectations. He was executed on the charge of being "king of the Jews." His entrance into Jerusalem for the final Passover was a royal one. According to the tradition, certain of his actions resulted in an attempt by the crowds to make him king (John 6:14–15). When he was arrested, at least one or two of his followers were bearing weapons. But the source material shows with a consistency and clarity which leave no room for doubt that Jesus did not entertain aspirations along these lines. His program was another. Indeed, on the contrary, his message *reversed* the popular dreams of how the ideal state of the future was to be brought about. His positive program—that the glorious future is not to be prepared for by overthrowing and plundering others, but by giving of, and sacrificing, oneself—will be analyzed a little later. But a few words must be said here about Jesus' and early Christi-

9

anity's salvation-historical and eschatological outlook, even though our treatment must be an abbreviated and simplified one.

For our purposes we may look at the eschatological discourse found in the three synoptic Gospels (Mark 13, Matthew 24, Luke 21), a text which evidently played an important role throughout the early church, though with considerable scope for variation in points of detail. Here the framework within which Jesus' followers live is sketched, and guiding counsels and warnings are given: this era is approaching its end; a fearful time of distress with all kinds of suffering is now at hand. In this situation Jesus' followers must know how they are to behave. The portrayal of the future given here leaves no room for a warlike intervention on Jesus' part to liberate his people, nor are they themselves to wage a holy war. Messianic figures will indeed arise, but such "liberators" are exposed in advance as false; the followers of Jesus are warned against heeding their summonses. The deliverance to be awaited will be brought about by a divine intervention from above. The Son of man will come on the clouds. The event will be as clear and unambiguous as the lightning which illuminates the sky. What will happen on that day will not be a messianic war of liberation or revenge. The Son of man will come to *hold judgment*. And the judgment is here depicted as being *universal*, an impartial examination of all peoples, including the people of God (cf. as well Matt. 7:21–23; 16:27; 25:31–46). (In certain other texts, the "faithful" escape the judgment.)

THE ATTITUDE TOWARD POLITICAL RULERS

Early Christianity was a minority movement lacking influence on the political plane. What was its attitude toward rulers?

Among the traditions of Jesus we find the pericope dealing with tribute to Caesar (Mark 12:13–17 par.). In it Jesus says, "Render to Caesar the things that are Caesar's, and to God the things that are God's" (RSV)—a saying which early Christianity thought was intended as a statement of principles. At its base is obviously the conviction that the emperor has a legitimate authority over his subjects, that he makes demands of obedience and loyal citizenship which even the "people of God" are bound to fulfill. The close of the saying, however, marks a limit: there is something which belongs exclusively to God and which he alone is to be given. If the demands of Caesar go against the "will of God," then he demands what God's people may not give him. A right to rebellion is not thereby conceded, but certainly the right—indeed, the duty—to disobey such laws and commands as violate God's will. The intention is no doubt that God's people on such occasions of conflict are to "obey God rather than men" (compare Acts 5:29) and take the consequences of punishment and suffering which follow.

The same basic attitude is expressed in Rom. 13:1–7. The theory that we are here dealing with an interpolation from a hand other than the apostle's is not supportable: all the evidence points to Paul as the source of the exhortations in these verses. But what he says could have been learned not only from the Jesus tradition (he does seem to allude to the saying about tribute which we have just cited) but also from earlier Jewish tradition on which both he and Jesus were dependent. Here is enjoined as a point of principle a general respect for, and loyalty toward, those in positions of authority in society. The Greek word *exousia* (which corresponds to the Hebrew *rashut*) means "rule," "authority" of any kind. The statement is formulated in a very general way: "Let every person (*pasa psychē*) be subject to the governing authorities. For there is no authority except from God, and those that exist have been instituted by God. Therefore he who resists the authorities resists what God has appointed" (RSV). The wording suggests that Paul is following traditional teachings. (Josephus expresses himself in similar terms: "No ruler comes to power apart from God," *War* 2.8.7. Compare also the wording in John 19:11.)

The same theme recurs in a number of other places in the early Christian documents, principally in 1 Tim. 2:1–3; Titus 3:1–2; 1 Pet. 2:13–17. With good reason it has been claimed that we are here dealing with a fairly fixed *topos* in the catechetical teaching of early Christianity (so E. G. Selwyn).

The New Testament statements we have noted are directed to Christian people and congregations in the Roman Empire and are intended to inculcate a proper attitude toward those in positions of political authority. They are thus not addressed to those authorities themselves. Nor do they provide a developed and detailed description of what political power really is, what position those in au-

11

thority actually possess, what their rights and obligations are, and how they are to exercise their power. If we are looking for this side of the matter, we must attempt to reconstruct the traditional ideological background which underlies such statements as we do find. To a certain extent, however, it is possible to do this.

According to the classical Old Testament outlook, wisdom, authority, and power—all forms of superiority—are divine. They belong to Yahweh: he and he alone allots them—sovereignly—to human beings (for example, Dan. 2:20–21). He is the one who allows some to "tend upward" and others to "tend downward," some to be "the head" and others "the tail," to use a few expressive phrases from Deuteronomy 28. It is Yahweh who makes one strong and another weak; it is he who gives one into the power of another. This applies to trials of strength between individuals as well as to those between groups and nations. It is Yahweh who raises up kings and deposes them. And it is he who permits first one kingdom, then another to extend its sovereignty in this world.

When thinking is developed strictly along these lines, divine blessing comes to be identified with power and superiority: wisdom, life, health, fertility, capacity to expand, success, victory. The various forms of weakness and inferiority are regarded as a divine curse: folly, sickness, infertility, setbacks, suffering, defeat, death (see especially Deuteronomy 28). As a rule, however, this way of thinking is not developed with complete consistency, particularly not in the postexilic period and early Judaism.

The idea that Yahweh gives power to rulers and those in authority is not, however, merely a theory of stations of power and rank among human beings. Always connected with the theme is the thought that those who receive power from God are at the same time entrusted with responsibility. They are given a *commission* and become—to a greater extent than other people—God's vice-regent and governor. Their authority is by no means a blank check for self-will and tyranny. Positions of power obligate: they are bound to their Commissioner to carry out the tasks demanded by their office, to perform their role with wisdom, righteousness, and mercy. Should they fail to do this, they are met with severe criticism by prophets and other people of God, and divine judgment is believed to hang over them. These views as to how rulers and others with authority are to appear and behave link up with traditional expectations directed toward those filling these roles; such expectations are made the basis of laws, commands, and ideals. The Holy Scriptures themselves are one of the important means by which these expectations are kept alive. Yet it is important to note that not only Israel's rulers and authorities but also the kings and lords of other nations were thought to be subject to the divine demands and to be accountable to heaven. Prophets like Amos severely condemn unjust acts of war and other violations of rights and righteousness perpetrated by nations other than Israel (for example, Amos 1:2—2:3; Obad. 1–16). Such wrongs stood under God's judgment even where Israel was not involved (Amos 2:1–3). Nor were such denunciations unwarranted. Bitter reminders of the demonic side of the political sphere were frequent.

A good ruler is seen as a blessing from God, an evil one as a punishment or trial. God himself is thought to look after the punishment of an unjust ruler, usually by raising up some "savior" (liberator) with the wisdom and strength to assemble people and lead them in victorious battle. At times even God's prophets inspire to revolt. When evil overreaches itself, the obligation of loyalty toward reigning rulers is broken and fixed instead on the ones expected to replace them. This psychology, which can be studied in both older (for example, Judges) and much later (the Books of the Maccabees) Jewish writings, cannot be pursued further here.

After the Exile, the conviction that Yahweh is God of all the earth grew in strength; this meant as well an increased faith in Yahweh as the one who enthrones and deposes kings. Closely connected with this is the conviction that Yahweh stands behind the laws of the nations. How did Jews living in the centuries surrounding Christ's birth view the latter?

Strongly Hellenized Jews (like the philosopher Philo) had assimilated the notions of popular Hellenistic philosophy concerning the "natural law" (*lex naturae*): a rational, divine law which permeates the whole universe. In good Hellenistic style, they viewed the laws and regulations of nations simply as explications, concrete manifestations of the one eternal, divine law. This was *one* way of developing the Old Testament concept of Yahweh as ruling creation and the nations.

But even Jews not so heavily influenced by Hellenism on this point might develop the ancient Jewish notions about the relations of rulers to the divine world and about the divine origin of the wisdom they needed. In Daniel we find many pregnant expressions of the relationship between the Most High and those to whom he entrusts power on earth. From the Book of the Wisdom of Solomon we may cite the following example:

> Listen therefore, O kings, and understand;
> learn, O judges of the ends of the earth.
> Give ear, you that rule over multitudes,
> and boast of many nations.
> For your dominion was given you from the Lord,
> and your sovereignty from the Most High,
> who will search out your works and inquire into your plans.
> Because as servants of his kingdom you did not rule rightly,
> nor keep the law,
> nor walk according to the purpose of God,
> he will come upon you terribly and swiftly,
> because severe judgment falls on those in high places.
>
> (6:1–5 RSV)

These are strains with which Hellenistic Jews were familiar but which even a Palestinian rabbi, for all his skepticism of "Greek" wisdom, might utter. What we have here is not the sublime notion of a *lex naturae* pervading the universe, but it is a firm belief that Yahweh assigns the rulers of the nations their tasks and obligations. Indeed, it is through these rulers, whose power and wisdom come from on high, that God intends to create relations of justice and mercy among human beings. Behind good laws stands the God of all goodness.

If we turn to the New Testament, we find there only insignificant traces of Hellenistic speculations about the natural law. But we do find—primarily, to be sure, as an assumption which leaves its mark without being the subject of specific treatment—a strong sense that God is at work even outside the boundaries of the chosen people, not least in the persons of rulers and authorities of various kinds. This consciousness lies behind the fact that Jesus and early Christianity recognize the emperor and Roman governors as legitimate earthly rulers and approve the administration and justice of the empire, being subject to them "not only to avoid God's wrath but also for the sake of conscience" (Rom. 13:5 RSV; cf. 1 Pet. 2:13). The brief hints given in Romans 13 and 1 Peter 2 indicate the task which the earthly authorities were thought to perform: the promotion of what is good and the hindering and punishing of what is evil. Probably Roman justice is intended also in 2 Thessalonians 2 in the mention of *to katechon*, "that which restrains" and keeps Antichrist and his forces of chaos from performing their work of destruction before the appointed time.

Jesus and his followers did not live in a democracy where the ordinary man has a share in the governing of society. Apart from isolated exceptions, they made up a minority in the Roman Empire without influence on the political plane. Nonetheless, their attitude of qualified loyalty toward the Roman authorities was not simply one of expedience; it was motivated by principles which they held. On the basis of early Christianity's eschatological outlook, they knew that they were living in a particular epoch of world history. The emperor and his rule were part of the unavoidable conditions of the end time. The Roman state found a place within the view of history which the church had inherited from older, apocalyptic streams (Daniel 7—12 and elsewhere) and given closer definition. According to this total view, it was not for Jesus and his followers to seek political power or to try to achieve their ends on that plane.

The powerful depiction of Jesus before Pilate in John's Gospel (chapters 18—19) has characteristics and peculiarities indisputably Johannine. But it does express the general view of early Christianity about Jesus' role and program: "My kingdom is not of this world." Jesus' rule is portrayed as heavenly, though it will one day be visibly established on earth as well. Still, while awaiting this divine "hour," the task for Jesus and his followers is not to make themselves lords and rulers by force and violence but, on the contrary, to empty themselves and sacrifice themselves. Not the rod of iron which crushes but the grain of wheat which dies is their symbol.

This does not mean that the political rulers are entirely left to themselves and their fate. In the Johannine scene (chapters 18—19) a motif typical of early Christianity is developed. Before Pilate, too, Jesus fulfills the task of "witnessing for the truth." In the very fact that one was brought before the authorities a divine purpose was seen: here was an opportunity "to bear testimony before them"

15

(Matt. 10:18 par.). Jesus was taken as a model, he "who in his testimony before Pontius Pilate made the good confession" (RSV). Before the mighty of this world, bold words were to be spoken of him who is "the King of kings and Lord of lords" (1 Tim. 6:12–16 and elsewhere). Though the essence of martyrdom could be found already in Judaism (2 Macc. 6:18–31; 7:1–41; 4 Maccabees 4—7, 8—17), it was in this Christian context that the word for "witness" (*martys*) soon came to mean "martyr."

Historically, the ethical teaching of the church through the ages has been strongest in the area of the individual's ethos, much weaker in that of society's, and weakest of all on the international level. This is no doubt partly due to the fact that the New Testament contains so little material dealing *directly* with questions of social ethics and still less dealing with relations between peoples and nations.

BIBLIOGRAPHICAL NOTE

The attitude toward the political "powers that be" has been the subject of lively study and debate. See, for example, Oscar Cullmann, *Jesus and the Revolutionaries* (New York: Harper & Row, Publishers, 1970); idem, *The State in the New Testament* (New York: Charles Scribner's Sons, 1956); Martin Hengel, *Was Jesus a Revolutionist?* (Philadelphia: Fortress Press, Facet Books, 1971); Ernst Käsemann, "Principles of the Interpretation of Romans 13," in his *New Testament Questions of Today* (Philadelphia: Fortress Press, 1969), pp. 196–216; idem, "Römer 13, 1–7 in unserer Generation," in *Zeitschrift für Theologie und Kirche 56* (1959): 316–76; Otto Ploeger, *Theocracy and Eschatology* (Richmond, Va.: John Knox Press), 1968; W. Schrage, *Die Christen und der Staat nach dem Neuen Testament* (Gütersloh: Gütersloher Verlagshaus G. Mohn, 1971). See further the note at the close of chapter two.

2

The Ethos of
the Jewish Theocracy

THE EMPHASIS ON SOCIAL ETHICS

The long centuries during which the Jews were subject to foreign
political powers did not lead to stagnation and sterility among
them; on the contrary, there was a marked spiritual development.
It was during this period that the Jewish theocracy took on its
characteristic form.

The Jewish people had a strong and positive self-awareness. According to the inherited self-understanding, Israel was the chosen
people, a people with whom the God of heaven had entered into a
covenant; the blessings and obligations of that covenant were to be
passed on and maintained from generation to generation (Gen.
18:18–19; Exod. 19:3–6; Deut. 4:7–10; 6:4–9; and so forth). During
the Exile, the awareness of this grew, and it left its indelible mark
on the work of consolidation which followed the national catastro-
phe. The Books of Ezra (especially chapters 7—10) and Nehemiah
(especially chapters 8—10 and 13) give quite a clear picture of the
general outlook and basic attitude involved. Under the wing of
foreign powers, the leading men of the Jews, "learned in the law of
the God of heaven," saw their task as organizing the people of God
and making them "a kingdom of priests and a holy nation."

The ethos which now took shape could not be based on any unified theoretical system developed with simple logic and consistency
by musing philosophers. The consolidation which followed the
Exile meant bringing together materials remarkably varied in their
nature and origin and assigning them a single, unified authority:
oracles which had been handed down, cultic and ritual rules, legal
material, prophetic sayings, collections of proverbs, hymns, psalms,

17

and prayers. The "Holy Scriptures" combined with oral traditions to form a great mosaic of sayings about life and life's many questions. All this now became a unit—achieved partly, to be sure, by means of censorship and new interpretations. The Jews did not distinguish between secular and religious law, between civil law and personal ethics, or between ceremonial and moral commands. All involved norms for life; and behind all these binding norms, the God of life was seen. "They come from One Shepherd."

As far as content is concerned, this didactic, normative material is strikingly comprehensive. If we compare the Old Testament with the New, we notice how strongly the New Testament concentrates on salvation and its consequences. In the Old Testament, all manner of questions touching human life are the subject of a treatment which is wide-ranging, diversified, and concrete. This is true of Jewish oral tradition as well. (There is thus good reason for the use of the Old Testament in the history of the Christian church not only as background to the New, but also as its necessary complement.) No attempt will be made here to describe the content of this comprehensive mosaic; the reader must be referred to the sources. I shall only draw attention to a few points which will serve as a basis for the presentation which follows.

A good deal of the Old Testament is addressed to the "people," as "brotherly" exhortation and teaching. But it is striking how much was originally intended for men in positions of authority—kings, princes, great men—or for leading, influential groups. This is why so much of it is concerned with the duties of those wielding power toward their subjects, the responsibility of the collective body toward the individual, the obligations of "the strong" toward "the weak." The emphasis on social ethics is quite apparent when the Old Testament is compared with the New.

One typical feature is that when Yahweh is depicted as the guarantor of justice, his concern for the weak and helpless is emphasized: for widows and fatherless, poor and strangers (for example, Exod. 22:21–27; Deut. 10:17–19; Psalm 146). Tyranny, outrage, and ruthlessness toward society's weaker members were often bitter realities in the ancient East. The powerful and influential could crush the insignificant by bribe or by threat even where due process of law was formally observed. Against all this the duty to maintain justice and incorruptible uprightness is strongly asserted. The exercise of justice is placed under the control and supervision of Yahweh. Judgments which are passed in Israel are Yahweh's judgments and must be irreproachable (Deut. 1:9–18; 16:18–20; 2 Chron. 19: 4–10; and so forth). Great value is placed on the ideal of being impartial (not "being afraid of the face of man," not having "respect of persons"). The strong and upright are to take an interest in, and secure the rights of, the weak and unprotected (Exodus 23; Leviticus 19, Deuteronomy 24; et passim). To "justify" someone means to secure justice for that person. It is unfortunately very difficult to know to what extent the priestly and prophetic teaching and the actual institution of laws really influenced the ongoing society of ancient Israel; probably, however, they did have a significant effect, especially in certain circles.

We may see in this demand for equality before the law the beginnings of a belief in human equality. Still, no illusions were entertained that all could have the same equipment, or that the conditions under which people live could ever be equal for all. Here bitter realities blocked the way: "The poor will never cease out of the land" (Deut. 15:11 RSV). What could be demanded was an identifying with, and concern for, those whose lot in life happened to be worse than one's own. This led to social laws and measures being enacted for the benefit of those who in one way or another had special needs: the sick and elderly, widows and orphans, poor and strangers. But it led as well to the creation of ideals of the righteous individual. Actually, such ideals were ancient, but the obligation to be oneself "righteous" (Hebrew saddiq, Greek dikaios) became more sharply focused at the time of an increasing awareness of the individual, which we can trace in postexilic Judaism. An ancient ideal as to how "the strong" should behave "when the Almighty is with him" (and thus provides him with the rich resources which accompany divine blessing) can be found in Job 29:

> I delivered the poor who cried,
> and the fatherless who had none to help him.
> The blessing of him who was about to perish came upon me,
> and I caused the widow's heart to sing for joy.
> I put on righteousness, and it clothed me;
> my justice was like a robe and a turban.

> I was eyes to the blind,
> and feet to the lame.
> I was a father to the poor,
> and I searched out the cause of him whom I did not know.
> I broke the fangs of the unrighteous,
> and made him drop his prey from his teeth.
>
> (29:12–17 RSV)

The strength of the strong, the wealth of the rich are not theirs solely for personal enjoyment. They are to be helpers of the needy. We might label this ideal "patriarchal benevolence."

Portrayals in which blessing and welfare are pictured as a general reality can be found, but they belong to dreams for the future, to expectations of the coming age of salvation when God will intervene in a radical way: "Then the eyes of the blind shall be opened, and the ears of the deaf unstopped; then shall the lame man leap like a hart, and the tongue of the dumb sing for joy . . ." (Isa. 35:5–6 RSV; cf. 29:17–24; 61:1–11). Seldom, however, do these expectations include those beyond the borders of the chosen people.

UNIVERSALISTIC TENDENCIES

The "universalism" of the Old Testament and postexilic Judaism is often exaggerated. It must be remembered that what we are dealing with is the religiously colored cultural heritage of a specific people of antiquity. Admittedly, the Israelite is often viewed there simply as human being; and to be sure, certain parts of the material were inspired from abroad, or even at times taken over from other peoples (especially, for example, a good deal of material in wisdom literature); but seldom is attention turned to what lies outside the bounds of the people and society of Israel. This is particularly noticeable in the laws and ethical rules. As a summary term for those toward whom the Israelite has obligations we often find the Hebrew word *rea*ʿ (Greek *ho plēsion*). This word means not "fellow man," but "neighbor," "associate," "brother," "fellow," "fellow countryman," and so forth. In legal texts, "fellow countryman" ("fellow Israelite") is, as a rule, the best translation. The command, "You shall love your neighbor as yourself" (Lev. 19:18 RSV), was understood by many as a summarizing formulation of the social and ethical duties of the Israelite. What was intended was thus not a universal love for people in general but loyal acceptance of responsibility toward one's fellow Israelites. A specific command required that "the stranger who sojourns with you"—in time this would be thought to refer to the full proselyte—"shall be to you as the native among you, and you shall love him as yourself" (Lev. 19:34 RSV; cf. Deut. 10:19); but this command in fact confirms that there were boundaries limiting the area within which such love was expected. The real stranger, the foreigner, is not intended. The ethos of the Jewish theocracy is thus not a universalistic one. Nonetheless, it does carry beneath its surface a profound universalism which needed only to be released. Individual Jewish prophets and teachers—especially when confronted by representatives of other peoples—have been able to perceive and give expression to this universalism. But something radical has to be done if it is to be brought into sharp focus.

One important prerequisite of universalistic views is the conviction that Yahweh is not only Israel's but the whole world's God, and that he has created everything. In this light, all creation assumes a unity when placed in relation to God; further, all humankind becomes one both in relation to the rest of creation and in relation to God. The creation narratives in Genesis 1—2, with the well-known formula that human beings are created in God's "image" and "likeness" (Hebrew *sælæm* and *d*ᵉ*mut*, LXX *eikōn* and *homoiōsis*), give expression to an outlook which would come to play a very important role in the advent of universalism and the recognition of human dignity; compare as well a text like Psalm 8. The idea that the God of heaven provides for all creation was also a factor tending to erase boundaries and broaden perspectives (cf. Psalms 104 and 145). The idea of a God who is "good to all, and [whose] compassion is over all that he has made" (Ps. 145:9) would sooner or later have to burst the bonds of narrow nationalism. Here too can be found a starting point for reflection about humankind's duties toward the nonhuman part of creation, particularly animals.

There is no question but that the increased sense of being a chosen people in covenant with God did tend to raise walls of demarcation between Jews and others and to restrict the scope of

21

Jewish vision. Still, a basis for universalistic tendencies did remain. Partly there was the fact that Israel's election was thought to have as its purpose the promotion of the whole world's redemption (cf. already Gen. 12:1–3). Then too, at the center of the obligations of the covenant were a small number of core commands pointing primarily to elementary duties of a quite general nature. Admittedly, the short, apodictically formulated commands of the Decalogue (see Exodus 20 and Deuteronomy 5) deal first with Israel's relationship with its God, Yahweh. Those duties toward neighbors which are mentioned in the second half are directed toward fellow Israelites: to honor one's (elderly) parents, to respect the life, marriage, possessions, and honor of one's fellow Israelite. But the command not to *worship* other gods would in time come to be taken as a direct *denial* of their existence, and the ideal relationship with one's fellow Israelite is formulated in such a general way that it could easily be extended to duties toward all people.

Bitter circumstances, however, prevented any straightforward development.

THE CONSEQUENCES OF
THE JEWISH CULTURAL STRUGGLE

In the Books of Ezra and Nehemiah we see a strong, programmatic attempt to separate Israel from foreign, "heathen" peoples. This attempt, however, does not seem to have been carried through with complete consistency; some freedom to be influenced by neighboring peoples apparently remained. A clear shift in the situation took place when the Syrian Seleucids took power over Palestine ca. 200 B.C. At this point certain Jewish groups began to promote enthusiastically assimilation with the Hellenistic world in which they found themselves. In addition, the hard hand of the foreign rulers began to make itself more keenly felt. In the 160s B.C., Antiochus Epiphanes set in motion his notorious measures of compulsion and violence in order to reshape Jewish society, forcing Jews to abandon their distinctiveness and to become a full-fledged part of his Hellenistic kingdom. Thus the inner Lebensraum of Jews was threatened. Jewish identity and distinctiveness were now the object of such an obvious and ruthless attack that there could be no doubt as to what was at stake. Nor did it require many summonses to battle to awaken in Jews conscious of their Israelite heritage a fanatic resistance. The Books of the Maccabees provide a clear picture of the cultural struggle (*Kulturkampf*) which now took shape. In the light of the threatening flame which had been kindled, everything native, everything inherited from the ancestors and genuinely Jewish appeared sacred and precious, to be preserved and protected at any price: the faith of the ancestors, their wisdom and teaching, their customs and habits, their laws, regulations, and institutions, and even the ancestral language, which had been falling into disuse. The holy motto became "zeal" (Hebrew *qinah*, Greek *zēlos*): zeal for God, zeal for his temple, zeal for the law (Torah), zeal for the tradition of the ancestors in its entirety. Jewish traditionalism—which, to be sure, had genuine and profound roots in the ancient covenant ideology—now began to take on its hard-wrought form. It was hammered into shape during a cultural struggle of life and death. A number of indomitable men, women, and young people went unhesitatingly to death for their faith (see, for example, 1 Macc. 2:31–38; 2 Maccabees 6—7; 4 Maccabees). These heroes became models—and not only for their contemporaries. Their memory was preserved. When vigilance waned and loyalty wavered, there was always someone to recall the pattern of struggle which had been set: where Jews had shed blood, Jews had binding obligations!

The cultural struggle kindled by the Maccabean revolt brought with it an impressive spiritual mobilization of the people: an awakening to consciousness, involvement, enthusiasm, and rallying around common ideals. In the process, the spiritual standards of the people were significantly raised. Community worship and teaching were intensified and consolidated. By means of the synagogues, communities throughout the country were reached. Earlier, education had been carried on in a tentative, nonsystematic way, with individual men of learning doing the teaching; now it would not be long before effective schools had begun to be built up in a programmatic way, apparently as a deliberate counter to the successful venture in training young people represented by the Hellenistic schools of their milieu (and even in Jerusalem). In the homes, attempts were made to create routines governing prayer life and religious instruction. The calendar of feasts gave the people the opportunity to assemble on festal occasions in Jerusalem in fuller force than before. The keeping of the Sabbath became an important act of religious confession.

In this situation, religious *experts* take on a more prominent role. Those with a command of the traditional holy law and familiar with sacred practice—the bearers of the tradition, "fathers"—are in great demand. Those learned in the Scriptures and wise men of other sorts now deliberately gather around them groups of disciples, large numbers of young people, indeed, crowds of all kinds. They are involved in teaching on a broad scale. But they attempt as well to rework and consolidate the system of norms contained in the binding sacred tradition. They gather, arrange, subdivide, clarify, sharpen, emphasize. The great quantity of "words" (commands, statutes) cannot be easily reduced to a harmonious unit. Many ancient statutes have lost their original meaning or become impractical; they must be reinterpreted. New problems require authoritative solutions. Such solutions are achieved by ingenious interpretations of the ancient holy writings and by the citing of precedents from the past. By means of this deliberate work—which is organized in a really effective way only after the catastrophes of A.D. 70 and 135—the inherited system of norms becomes more comprehensive, detailed, and specific than ever before.

This summoning of spiritual strength, this intensive rallying around the native heritage of the people of God, carries with it certain consequences which it is important to note. Some of these will be mentioned here at the same time as I attempt to characterize the ethos which emerges.

First we must note that because of the cultural struggle, the genuine heritage from the fathers is given a more *exclusive* worth than it had before. Creative association with neighboring peoples— both giving and taking—becomes more difficult than it once had been. That which exists outside the walls is thought to pose a threat of annihilation; naturally, it is difficult to see what is hostile in any appreciative light. Then too, the inheritance from the fathers becomes more fixed than before. Even internal attempts at renewal and reform appear risky. Loyalty toward the holy heritage becomes strict, uncompromising. Conservatism increases. Admittedly, perceptive and original rabbis were able to take measures which were renewing and creative. But such measures always had to be motivated with a reference to what was old and acknowledged, even if it meant resorting to extremely far-fetched interpretations of Scripture and strained citations of precedents from the tradition. Anything new had to be introduced as a legitimate growth, an expression of something actually present, though concealed, in the sacred wording, or as a rediscovery of something which had been forgotten at some point in the past during a dark period of Israel's history.

The ethos which thus takes shape is designed to bring unity and uniformity to the behavior of the people of God. In the process, the scope of individual freedom diminishes. A network of sacral regulations is laid over every facet of life. In every situation in life it becomes necessary to recognize and respect the difference between what a holy people may do and what it may not, between the permitted and the forbidden, the clean and the unclean. The authoritative men, "judges," "scribes," "sages," rabbis who declared the binding rules of life (halakha) could, at least in certain circles, be extremely strict. This was true at Qumran, where the boundaries of the community of the faithful were clearly demarcated. But the majority of "scribes" were concerned for the training of the people as a whole, claiming that though there was indeed a need to observe the law carefully, the demands of the law must still be made to appear reasonable and practicable. This was the way Pharisaic scribes—especially certain of them—reasoned. One of the leading principles of the school of Hillel was that the law was never to be interpreted in a way more strict or burdensome than was absolutely necessary.

It is difficult to avoid the conclusion that the ethos of the people of God becomes more intellectual and nomistic under these conditions than it had been before. The prescribed program is one of activities. God's people are to repent and to show their zeal in behaving loyally, courageously, perseveringly. God's will as revealed to the ancestors is to be *done*. To be done, it must also be known. The one who would fulfill obligations must receive training and instruction. Hillel's saying that "an ignorant man cannot be saintly" (*Abot* 2:5) expresses an important point in this context. The one who would be "righteous" must acquire no small amount of learning.

The commands which had to be learned and observed were many. But those who undertook the demanding course of Torah study have not left us sighs and laments at the quantity and weight of the commands. On the contrary, "joy in the law," enthusiasm, and pride are what stand out about these "zealots of the law": pride that Israel had been privileged to know God's will, not simply in rough outline but in every detail of life. Furthermore, because the commands were so many, Israel had the opportunity to procure great "reward" by keeping them. In principle, every command was to be kept. To be sure, there was some disagreement as to the exact scope of the Torah. The Sadducees, for example, denied that *unwritten* (that is, only orally transmitted) laws could have any claim to be God's Torah. Still, those laws acknowledged to be a part of the divine Torah had to be faithfully observed.

Inevitably, the ethos which took shape under these conditions assumed in many cases the character of a formal observance of commands, the need and motivation for which were not apparent. In new situations, many ancient commands appeared incomprehensible or meaningless. But they could not simply be abolished. A saying of Rabban Jochanan ben Zakkai (latter half of the first century A.D.) about one of Torah's purity regulations is typical: "A dead body does not convey uncleanness, nor does water bring [ritual] purity, but the Holy One, blessed be He, has said: 'I have laid down a statute and made a decree . . .' and you are not allowed to transgress my decree" (*Num.Rab.* 19.8 par.). The saying indicates that obedience toward the inherited commands often had to be purely formal, without any basis in one's own sense of right and wrong. Had something else been commanded, one's duty would have been to do that instead.

The rabbis were, however, aware of the inherent risk of a superficial conformity with the law and of its mechanical fulfillment. Hence they stressed in a number of different ways the necessity of fulfilling the many statutes "from the heart." An original concept, and one difficult to convey in any simple way in English, is their

demand for the heart's *kawwanah*: God's commands are to be fulfilled with *kawwanah*, "inwardness." By this term they meant the
heart's genuine desire to do what God has commanded, an inner
commitment to what one does in obedience to God's law.

The rabbis' stress on the "inwardness" of true obedience to the
law was *one* way of linking up with the many Old Testament texts
which indicate that God's will is to rule in man's "heart," and particularly with the statements indicating that God one day in the
future would pour out his Spirit over his people and write his law
in their heart (for example, Jer. 31:31–34; Ezek. 11:17–21; 36:22–
32; Joel 2:27–29). Naturally, ideals for the future were influenced
by prophetic words of this kind about a coming day of salvation
and perfection, in which each individual member of God's people
would be directly related to God and would possess a mature and
independent faculty for discerning the demands of God's will.

SIMPLIFYING, DEEPENING,
AND INDIVIDUALIZING THE COMMANDS

Efforts to preserve and apply the great quantity of commands—
each and every one of them—and to regulate the lives of God's people in every detail could not prevent questions as to the basis and
purpose of the whole endeavor. Reflections of this nature were
inevitable. There was also a need for simple rules of thumb by
which people could get at least a rough grasp as to what it was God
demanded of his children (cf. already such texts as Mic. 6:8). Moreover, confrontations with foreign sages and others from without
created a need for short answers indicating what Jewish "wisdom"
was really all about. Especially among those whose interest in ritual
matters was limited if not extinguished, we find attempts being
made to provide brief summaries of Torah's content. It is undoubtedly no coincidence that we encounter such tendencies at an
early period among Jews subject to Hellenistic influence (Tob.
4:15; *Letter of Aristeas* 207; Philo in Eusebius, *Praeparatio Evange-
lica* 8:7; and *b. Šabb.* 31a, where Hillel is confronted by a prospec-
tive proselyte). "The golden rule" ("Whatever you wish that men
would do to you . . ."), which here is formulated in different ways,
need not in itself have been adopted from a Hellenistic source. It is

rather a development of the practical implications of Lev. 19:18. The formulation there could be taken in two ways: "You shall love your neighbor as yourself" or "You shall love your neighbor; [he is] as you." When this command is extended in Lev. 19:34 to include the stranger living among the Israelites, this is done with a reference to their similar lots: the Israelites too have been "strangers" in a foreign country. Such a reference certainly led thoughts in the direction of maxims like the golden rule. One thing in any case is clear: when one reasons in this way, demands of ritual peculiar to, and distinctive of, Israel have been disregarded. Interest is concentrated on obligations toward those with whom one comes in contact. If these obligations are applied in a profound way to the individual, it becomes natural to extend and generalize them.

It is, however, a mistake to think that a rabbi intended to *replace* Torah with a brief maxim. No rabbi felt free to dismiss a single one of God's commands. A short maxim (referred to as a k^elal-saying) was intended only as a handy summary, a pocket-size compendium. Hillel is reported to have said of the golden rule, "This is the whole of Torah; the rest is simply commentary." But he adds, significantly enough, "Go and study [Torah in its entirety]!"

Efforts to focus attention on the fundamental demands of the law took many forms. We are told—and it is not improbable—that in the temple and even in certain circles outside Jerusalem the Decalogue (the Ten Commandments) was recited daily in New Testament times, a custom apparently broken off at the time of the struggles with early Christianity. An ancient text given still greater weight was the *Shema* (made up of Deut. 6:4–9; 11:13–21; Num. 15:37–41). During the centuries in which Jews were subject to foreign powers, they continually had to remind themselves of their citizenship above, "citizenship in heaven." It became the duty—just when, we cannot say—of each Jewish man every morning and evening to consecrate himself and remind himself of his true condition. He had to "take upon himself the yoke of the reign of heaven," to confess that he, with Israel as a whole, stood in a covenant relationship with the God of heaven, by reciting the *Shema*. And this text had become the object of much reflection (see, for example, *m. Ber.* 9:5).

28

In the *Shema*, the words whose supreme importance is incomparable come first:

> Hear, O Israel: The Lord our God is one Lord;
> and you shall love the Lord your God
> with your whole heart,
> and your whole soul,
> and your whole strength . . .

This confession of the world's true Sovereign expresses an outlook which is fundamental: one God holds sway over the whole world, and "God's children" are to love him with everything they are and have. This outlook is characterized by its all-encompassing, unified nature. It is probable that the words "with your whole heart, and your whole soul, and your whole strength" were originally intended to be taken together as one all-inclusive, abundant formula rather than each part by itself. But in the late postexilic period it had become natural to examine each detail of the wording of holy texts in an attempt to define the special significance which underlay each particular. Some rabbis used to point out that "Torah speaks in the language of men" and can therefore allow itself superfluous words, but for most it was self-evident that God never says an unnecessary word. Hence they tried to discover the special teaching which details of the texts might be intended to convey in addition to the meaning of the text as a whole.

On the basis of the two imperatives "Hear!" and "You shall love!" —as well as other important texts—it was natural to point to obedience and love as fundamental divine demands. To obey (expressed with the Hebrew verb *shama'*, "hear," "listen," "obey") here means to listen effectively; that is, to hear and behave in accordance with what one hears. In fact the two demands were seen to combine into a single command: love for God primarily means obeying his will.

The Hebrew word for "love" (*ahav*) has a more robust significance than our word in English. It refers rather to an attitude and a manner of behaving than to a feeling. This is why love can be *commanded*. To "love God" means to treat him as God: trust him, obey him, show loyalty to him—whatever he sends and whatever he demands. The words "with your whole heart" indicate that one's

29

attitude toward God is to be wholehearted and undivided, having its foundation in the center of one's personality. (The "heart" signified one's innermost being, the center of one's thoughts, will, feelings, and instincts.) To "love God with one's whole heart" was a standard expression for a proper relationship with God (see especially Deuteronomy).

The scribes—especially Pharisaic scribes, whose heritage the rabbis later developed—found significant the fact that the love command also emphasizes the "soul" and "strength." They concluded that God intended to specially emphasize two other aspects to one's love for him. "With your whole soul" was taken to mean "even if he takes your soul," that is, even if he requires that you face death for his sake. One is not to renounce the good and proper allegiance God demands in order to escape death. "With your whole strength" was explained as meaning "with all your *mamon*." The word *mamon* covers all one's possessions which go beyond life and the body itself; that is, all one's resources (property and wealth and the power and status which accompany wealth). "With your whole strength" thus indicated that even one's desire for wealth and power must be subject to the discipline of God's commands and of secondary importance. In this way a superb summary was sketched of what it means to "take up the yoke of the reign of heaven." It means to love God with everything one is and has, even at the cost of life itself.

But when the heavenly demands are interpreted in this way, the ethos of the theocracy has been transformed into the ethos of the children of God, the secret of which lies not in external laws and ritualized patterns of behavior but in people's hearts. It has been individualized. It is perfectly clear that Jesus and early Christianity were able to associate themselves with efforts directed along these lines, and hence that even Jesus himself listened in a positive way to scribes who were "not far from the kingdom of God" (Mark 12:34). Still, the fact remains that "the Pharisees and scribes" were concerned above all to teach the people a holy, authoritative praxis, a regulated way of life (halakha). That this program could become a façade, an empty routine replacing the living devotion of God's children toward their God and fellow human beings, is evidenced by, among other things, the internal critique brought by the rabbis themselves. The bitter struggle with Pharisaism in which early Christians found themselves has, however, had the effect of silencing and eliminating to a large extent such words of appreciation as might have been directed toward their rivals. There are greater similarities between the scribes and Jesus in terms of ethical teaching than one would be aware of on the basis of the criticism of "hypocrisy" (*hypokrisis*) found in the Gospels.

BIBLIOGRAPHICAL NOTE

For a general study of the outlooks treated in chapters one and two, the following works may be recommended: Elias Bickerman, *From Ezra to the Last of the Maccabees: Foundations of Post-Biblical Judaism* (New York: Schocken Books, 1962); Rudolf Bultmann, *Primitive Christianity in its Contemporary Setting* (Philadelphia: Fortress Press, 1980); Martin Hengel, *Jews, Greeks and Barbarians: Aspects of the Hellenization of Judaism in the Pre-Christian Period* (Philadelphia: Fortress Press, 1980); idem, *Judaism and Hellenism: Studies in Their Encounter in Palestine During the Early Hellenistic Period* (Philadelphia: Fortress Press, 1974; 1 vol. ed., Fortress Press, 1981; London: SCM Press, 1981); Joachim Jeremias, *Jerusalem in the Time of Jesus: An Investigation into Economic and Social Conditions During the New Testament Period* (Philadelphia: Fortress Press, 1969); H. G. Kippenberg, *Religion und Klassenbildung im antiken Judäa: Eine religionssoziologische Studie zum Verhältnis von Tradition und gesellschaftlicher Entwicklung* (Göttingen: Vandenhoeck & Ruprecht, 1978); J. Leipoldt and W. Grundmann, *Umwelt des Urchristentums*, vols. 1–3 (Berlin: Evangelische Verlagsanstalt, 1967–72); Bo Reicke, *The New Testament Era: The World of the Bible from 500 B.C. to A.D. 100* (Philadelphia: Fortress Press, 1968); Emil Schürer, *The History of the Jewish People in the Age of Jesus Christ (175 B.C.–A.D. 135)*, revised and edited by Geza Vermes and Fergus Millar (Edinburgh: T. & T. Clark, 1973–). See also the bibliography at the close of this book.

3

Early Christianity's Ethos
According to Matthew

INTRODUCTION

A sure way to cut oneself off from any possibility of understanding the structure of Jesus' and early Christianity's ethos is to begin with the slogan "Behold, I make all things new." Our sources speak an altogether different language. Nowhere in the New Testament documents is it said that Jesus came to the people of God in order to do something *fundamentally* new. Nowhere is it supposed that the Eternal God has hitherto surrounded himself with silence, his will first being revealed when Jesus' voice is heard in Israel. At the base of the whole New Testament are the convictions that God has created the world, that he each moment sustains it, that he has made himself known, that his will has been proclaimed to Israel's forebears and preserved by the covenant people in the Holy Scriptures and in other "words" from the ancestors. The evangelists do not depict Jesus as one who called upon his people to radically deny their ancient faith, abandon their ancient obligations, and adopt something completely new. He summons them rather to accept the good news that the reign of heaven is at hand—the prophetic message that the hour is near when it will become apparent that "the Lord is *one*"—and, in view of the impending crisis, to rightly understand and rightly observe that divine will which God's people have already been given, though not in its final, "fulfilled" form. Jesus could have based his teaching on a text like Deut. 30:11–14 without any hesitation.

Following in the footsteps of Johannes Weiss and Albert Schweitzer, New Testament exegetes of this century have emphasized strongly that Jesus' message about God's reign is an *eschato-*

33

logical message, that it relates to something which has never before existed and which even now is only in the offing (*im Kommen*). In this they make an important observation. But if one develops it one-sidedly—as Schweitzer and many others with him have done— one ends up with a kind of Marcionism which imposes a rather heavy-handed treatment on the sources. It is quite clear that Jesus does not speak of the reign of God (or heaven) only as something future. In a manner which links up with traditional ideology, he often speaks of God's reign as something which exists now and which has existed in the past. God may have decisive plans for the future, but he reigns and exercises his dominion in the present too. This must be borne in mind, especially in interpreting Jesus' and early Christianity's ethos. To be sure, the eschatological perspectives clearly have an influence on how "God's will" is interpreted: the demands become sharper and more intense in times of crisis. But it is equally clear that they do not bring about a break with what God has required of his people in the past. A statement like "I have come not to abolish . . . but to fulfill" (Matt. 5:17 RSV) may be taken as a methodological guidepost.

Here—not least because of the precarious situation in which the debate on the historical reliability of the Gospels now finds itself— I shall not attempt to derive Jesus' own ethos from the interpretation which the early Christians put on it. With a view to simplicity, I take up three of the interpretations of Jesus which we find between the covers of the New Testament, emphasizing chiefly the ethical side of their presentations. My reasons for choosing Matthew, Paul, and John have already been indicated (see above, Introduction).

THE DIVISION BROUGHT ABOUT
BY JESUS

At the center of Matthew's interest is not Jesus' message, but Jesus himself. The First Gospel is strongly Christocentric. As far as Jesus' message is concerned, Matthew summarizes it with the words "Repent, for the reign of heaven is at hand" (4:17; cf. 10:7). These words express something central to the gospel: a decisive point in the history of redemption has now come; this must be realized and appropriate action taken.

At the heart of Matthew's Gospel lies the so-called parable chapter, a chapter which deals with "the secrets of the reign of heaven" (13:1–52). This passage treats the response God's word receives when it is now proclaimed for the people of God by Jesus Christ and his messengers. Those whose response is analyzed are the covenant people, the citizens of the reign of heaven, Israel. Since in reacting to the "word of the reign" they take a position on what is proclaimed as right and good, we have here a text of fundamental importance for an understanding of the realm of ethics in Matthew.

The "word" is said to divide its hearers into two categories: some are open to it and receive it, others harden themselves completely or are only superficially and temporarily receptive. This division into two groups is not, however, something radically new. What happens is simply that an already existing—though concealed—division is brought to light; indeed, the lines become fixed and final.

Where are the lines drawn? "Those who have" are divided from "those who do not have." When the divine message is now proclaimed, "it is given" to those who have, but not to those who do not. The difference between the two groups is thereby radicalized. "Those who have" become richer, to the point of overflowing (*perisseuein*). "Those who do not have" are forced to take a position which leaves them still poorer than they were. They lose even the little they may have had. How is this to be understood?

The chapter contains seven real parables. One of these is in a class by itself. It is placed first and is commented upon and interpreted at length. Moreover, the other six parables seem to build further on its base, only supplementing what is said in it. I am referring to the parable of the sower.

The parable itself (vv. 3–9) tells how the sower sows his seed on four types of soil. He sows along the pathway, on rocky ground, among thorns, and on good soil. In the first three cases, the sowing is unsuccessful, but in the fourth case it has its intended result. In the interpretation which is provided (vv. 18–23), the parable is said to deal with the fate which "the word of the reign" (that is, of the reign of heaven) encounters in four types of hearers. How are they described?

The first type (vv. 4 and 19) is "the one sown along the path." Such people hear the word but do not "understand." The evil one thus has no problem in snatching the word from their "hearts."

The second type (vv. 5–6 and 20–21) is "the one sown on the

rocky ground." This person hears the word and receives it enthusiastically but falls away when tribulation or persecution arises on account of the word.

The third type (vv. 7 and 22) is "the one sown among the thorns." This person hears the word but allows the worries of this age and the allurement of riches to choke it, with the result that fruit is never borne.

Finally, the fourth type (vv. 8 and 23) is "the one sown on the good soil." Such people hear the word and "understand" and therefore bear fruit as well, that is, *act* upon it. Their yield may be hundredfold, sixtyfold, or thirtyfold.

The decisive line is drawn between those who bear no fruit (types one to three) and the one who does (type four). Note that the main interest in the parable is devoted to the former category. Within it three different types are described, and described in some detail. To be sure, within the latter category (type four, those who prove true) there is an intimation of three subdivisions (note the figures one hundred, sixty, and thirty), but no further details are given, either in the parable or in the interpretation. This observation underlines something apparent from the context in which the parable is placed as well. What is reflected on here is the problem presented by the *unfaithful*, not that of the faithful. The parable of the sower is not a concise treatment of the life and situation of Jesus and his disciples. It is primarily a brief, well-thought-out text dealing with those who reject Jesus' message of the reign; that is, those who do not qualify as "children of the reign": the Israel which does not become the church.

The parable of the sower occupies—as far as I can see—a central position in the Gospel of Matthew. The evangelist and that line of tradition which he primarily represents have obviously used this parable as a key to the entire tradition of Jesus. Taking their categories from it, they have examined Jesus' own exemplary—so early Christianity saw it—way of being and behaving, the *problematical* (not yet "perfect") attitudes and behavior of Jesus' followers, and the *reprehensible* stance of his opponents. I must here limit myself to certain aspects of the wide-ranging problems into which the parable is meant to give adequate insight.

In the parable, the sower is said to sow; in the interpretation, he sows "the word of the reign." The *content* of this word is not subjected to further interpretation. Attention is focused instead on the reactions of those who hear it.

The structure of the parable suggests that the fate of the sowing depends primarily on the nature of the soil. Other factors are secondary. It is the condition of the soil which allows the birds, the sun's heat, and the thorns to have their devastating effects. When the soil is as it should be, the seed bears fruit. The structure of the parable is well maintained in the interpretation. The prime reason that the word does not have its intended effect is (1) that people's hearts are hardened so that they do not "understand," (2) that people are so "rootless" and unstable that they cannot withstand suffering and martyrdom for the sake of the word, and (3) that people allow themselves to be enticed by riches and anxieties. When the word does have its intended effect, the primary reason for this is (4) that people "hear, understand, and therefore also act" upon what they have heard. Other factors are secondary: when people hear without "understanding," the devil can snatch the word from their hearts; when people are "rootless" and unstable, persecution can lead to apostasy; when people are entangled in riches and worldly cares, mammon and anxiety can choke the word. But when people are as they should be, these negative factors cannot hinder the power of the word: the yield of fruit is enormous, the harvest great.

The basic thought of the parable is thus that the condition of human beings—not here their natural disposition, but rather what we would call their spiritual or moral condition—is determinative. This is what is meant by "having" and "not having." External circumstances are not decisive. Human beings are presented in this parable as *responsible*.

Note especially the pattern used as a basis for examining the attitude of God's people toward the "word of the reign." It is none other than the text which indicated what the "yoke of the reign of heaven" specifically involved: the summarizing credal text, the weightiest command of the law—the beginning of the *Shema* (Deut. 6:4–5). According to the parable, the divine word is proclaimed in vain to those who do not love God (1) with their whole heart, (2) with their whole soul, and (3) with their whole strength, but it is proclaimed with success for the true Israelites who do (4). With the proclamation of Jesus, then, the true citizens of the reign of heaven are separated from those who only apparently are "children of the reign."

In Mark's version (4:20), those represented by the good soil are said to hear the word, *receive* it, and bear fruit. Matthew has put the matter more precisely. For the vague term "receive" (*paradechesthai*) he has substituted the more specific word "understand" (*synienai*). By this he means the existential understanding which involves both comprehension and agreement, the "Aha!" experience in which one comes to a positive insight as to what the matter is all about and accepts it for positive reasons.

Matthew has reflected a good deal about the "insight" which is involved and committed (verb: *synienai*). In his view, the *great* divide among the people of God separates those whose hearts are hardened on the one hand from those who "understand" and, as a result, pattern their lives according to the heavenly proclamation. Mark presents the disciples in several places as not understanding what Jesus says and does during his earthly ministry. Matthew most often corrects this. According to Matthew, the disciples do "understand"—though at times insufficiently and with difficulty (for example, 16:5–12). What they lack during Jesus' earthly activity is a full measure of faithfulness and confidence (*pistis*): they are still "of little faith" (but not "unbelieving" like the others, 13:58; 17:17).

THE RIGHTEOUSNESS THAT "OVERFLOWS"

As we have already noted, the parable of the sower focuses attention on the three types of hearers who do not receive the word of the reign in a proper, enduring way. Those, on the other hand, who do this (type four) are treated summarily. They are said to "understand and therefore also bear fruit, and yield a hundredfold, or sixty, or thirty." What this means is not developed but can be deduced with the help of the strict construction of the parable. Hundredfold fruit is borne by those who understand the word with an obedient "heart" and conduct themselves so in accordance with God's will that they not only sacrifice all their possessions (their "strength") but even their ultimate asset, life itself (their "soul"), for him: the martyrs. Those who bear sixtyfold have an obedient heart and sacrifice all their possessions but are not compelled to give up their lives for the sake of the word. Thirtyfold fruit is borne by those whose heart is just as undivided and obedient but who are not compelled either to sacrifice their lives or to renounce all their possessions for God's sake.

Thus the word of the reign, when sown by Jesus (and his messengers), is said to bear rich fruit among those represented by the good soil. The same point is made when they are said to "have abundance" (*perisseuein*, v. 12). What this abundance of righteousness consists of is treated clearly and in detail in another important Matthean text, 5:17–48. Here it is said in the introduction (vv. 17–20) that people cannot "enter the kingdom of heaven" unless their righteousness "abundantly overflows" (*perisseuein*) in comparison with that of the scribes and Pharisees. And in the examples which follow (vv. 21–48) we are given a closer description of this "overflowing" righteousness. Notice how, even in the final example (v. 46), the thought is clearly expressed that one must do something "overflowing," something which "exceeds" (*perisson*), if one is to receive a "reward" in heaven.

The examples given are introduced by the formula "You have heard that it was said (to the men of old) . . ." (RSV). This formula is followed each time by an Old Testament command taken in its literal sense. We are here confronted with a series of commands as to how, according to the scribes and Pharisees, the "children of the reign of heaven" are to *act*. The commandments demand righteous *action*: you shall not commit murder, adultery, or perjury; you shall not demand a punishment more severe than the crime; you shall love (take care of) your "neighbor" (friend, compatriot). This is contrasted in each case with an authoritative statement of Jesus, introduced by the phrase "But I say to you . . ." These statements sharpen what is demanded and suggest an *inner attitude* which goes infinitely further than the action dealt with by the commandment: you are not even to get angry with your brother, not to commit adultery with a woman even in your heart, not to resort to the expedient of an oath. You are not to take any action at all when wronged; your love is to include even your enemies and persecutors.

Here the demands have been removed from the plane of action

to that of the heart. What is depicted is a total attitude, the secret of which lies in the fact that God's children, from their heart, wholly and undividedly, love God and their fellow human beings with a love which includes action. It is a living, consistent, total attitude.

We can see as well the principle of interpretation that has been used in the description of "overflowing" righteousness. The question has been put to each command: how is this command fulfilled by the one who loves God with his whole heart, soul, and strength (*mamon*)? The law's greatest command (Deut. 6:4-5) has added depth to the others, has filled them with its own weighty content (cf. Matt. 22:34-40).

Significant too is the fact that the examples conclude with the "second" command which is "like the first," that of love for one's neighbor (Lev. 19:18). The Old Testament commandment—as we have already pointed out—does not demand a general love for all people, but a loyal acceptance of responsibility toward one's fellow Israelite. A special command prescribed that the same love was to include "the stranger who sojourns with you" (Lev. 19:34 RSV; cf. Deut. 10:19) but did not take in foreigners in general. Admittedly, a certain compassion and helpfulness toward enemies was enjoined in the law (Exod. 23:4-5), and exemplary stories of "good Samaritans" were passed on (2 Chron. 28:5-15), but all this was kept within quite modest boundaries. Advocates could even be found for a "love" toward enemies which was motivated by the desire for revenge (Prov. 25:21-22), something which, in certain pious circles, could be developed into a conscious program (Qumran). When Jesus commands that love be shown even to "enemies" and "persecutors," he goes radically beyond the boundaries mentioned by the literal command of the traditional law. Now the demand is that one love everybody, even those who least deserve it. The heart is to have place for but a single spirit, that of love. Its attitude thus becomes a consistent one. And the "overflow" streams out to all.

The examples taken up in the antitheses are—with one possible exception (vv. 33-37)—commands which deal with one's relations to other *human beings*; nonetheless, they are sharpened by means of the command to love *God*. This illustrates the fundamental principle that a proper relationship toward God carries with it a proper attitude toward one's fellow humans: the children of God's reign are not to be individuals who, egocentrically and in isolation from others, develop their own personalities before God, but loyal citizens of the reign of God, taking their part in its fellowship.

In the interpretation of the commands in 5:17–48, we see that the traditional observance of the law, while not regarded as wrong, is thought to be insufficient. The literal demands of the law are perceived as incomplete. Further, we see that in this new interpretation the demands are not only sharpened but also brought to converge. They tend to unite into a single demand, that of a pure and undivided, loving heart. It is typical that the section concludes with a concise and comprehensive demand: "You, therefore, must be perfect (*teleioi*), as your heavenly Father is perfect" (v. 48 RSV). The term *teleios* (Hebrew *tamim* or *tam*) means complete, undamaged, undivided, and unimpeachable in the attitude of one's heart and, as a result, in all one's doings before God and men, "perfect."

THE LAW'S CONCRETE COMMANDMENTS

In Matthew's Gospel, the idea that Jesus defied, revoked, or abolished Torah, in whole or in part, is dismissed. It is explicitly said that he did not come to "abolish" (*katalyein*) but to "fulfill" (*plēroun*) (5:17). What is said in 5:18–19 about the necessity of maintaining, in teaching and practice, even the least of the commandments is regarded by many scholars as secondary. The form of these verses is strikingly technical and rabbinic; moreover, it is far from easy to see how their content can be harmonized with certain other sayings of Jesus and traditions about his conduct. Whatever the truth of the matter, one thing is both clear and of great importance for the person interested in Matthew's line of reasoning: the Christian scribe who here interprets Jesus acquits him wholly of the charge of wanting to "abolish" any of the law's commands. On the other hand, Jesus has, in his view, followed a generally accepted juridical axiom: that fundamental law takes precedence over all other law; that each individual statute and paragraph must give expression to the demand and spirit of that fundamental law. Since the legal experts of the Jews saw in God's law a great unity, this axiom became for them the principle that "weightier" commands, when in conflict with "lighter" commands, take precedence over them. According to Matthew, Jesus has adopted this principle; he has simply pursued it in an extraordinarily radical way.

In preceding chapters we attempted to characterize the Jewish program of Torah-centered piety. Israel is to keep in mind the obligation to be a holy people and hence to guard God's law earnestly and diligently: to study it and apply it in every circumstance of life. This program had its consequences. The holy nation separated itself from Gentiles, the righteous distanced themselves from sinners. The walls which were thus raised were based primarily on demands for holiness and on particular observances in which obedience was shown and faith confessed.

If we look at how the Matthean Jesus is portrayed, we get the impression that he has no great respect for statutes which erect walls of this kind. He goes to the "lost," to "sinners," "unclean," those who do not know the law and as a result do not follow it. In order to associate with such people, he has to set himself above prescriptions of purity which would prevent it (9:9–13). When his hungry disciples do a little "work" in order to get some food on the Sabbath, he does not intervene and stop them with a reminder that this conflicts with the Sabbath command (12:1–8). He heals the chronically ill on the Sabbath, in spite of the fact that this requires a "work" which, according to the traditional Sabbath rules, must be put off till the following day (12:9–14). He obviously feels that the law does not hinder his "doing good" toward others (cf. 12:12).

Typical too is the sequence which Matthew reveals. The picture we get is not that of a man who first propounds a theory and then demonstrates it in action. Here the actual attitude and action come first: a man acts positively and with generosity toward the people around him. It is when his behavior is challenged as problematic that it has to be explained. The arguments to which he then resorts allow us to perceive something of the secret behind his conduct. The principle adopted is that the weightiest demands of the law must be met first of all and that the lesser commands have to give way in order to make this observance of the law's fundamental demands possible. The statutes which are pushed to the side are those prescribing ritual activities and particular observances. Even the

Sabbath command scarcely holds its own, in spite of the fact that it is part of the Decalogue and that its observance had virtually become a confession of Israel's faith. The statements made in 12:8 and 12:12 mean that the Sabbath command—the command to *rest* on the seventh day—is nearly rendered inoperative. At the time of the evangelist, Jewish Christians evidently observed the Sabbath. Later, however, they ceased to do so, and the development is quite understandable.

In the anti-Pharisaic discourse in chapter 23 too we see how a similar development is set in motion. The rule given in vv. 2–3 enjoins loyalty and obedience toward the demands made by those occupying "Moses' seat" (the "scribes and Pharisees"). But these authorities are subjected to a blistering critique—a critique based on, among other things, an imputed insensibility toward what is more and what is less important in the law. Their observance of the law's lesser demands is not in itself dismissed, but what is demanded first of all is an observance of "the weightier matters of the law" (*ta barytera tou nomou*): here *krisis*, *eleos*, and *pistis*, that is, justice, mercy (love for one's fellow human being), and faithfulness, are listed. These weighty demands—demands placed on the heart, which govern, or have consequences for, one's total attitude toward one's fellow human beings—are to take precedence over concerns about tithing "mint and dill and cummin" (v. 23). Those who earnestly pursue purity are not to "strain out a gnat and swallow a camel [when they drink out of a cup]," as one saying aptly puts it (v. 24).

In 15:1–20, certain purity regulations are discussed in a passage thoroughly worked over by the evangelist. The Pharisees and scribes are accused of rendering God's own commands inoperative (*akyroun*) by means of their statutes; that is, they show no awareness of what the really fundamental commandments demand or of the priority they should receive. The principle then propounded is that nothing from outside which enters one's mouth (that is, no food) can defile one before God (v. 11). A person becomes unclean before God because of the uncleanness of the "heart," and *only* that of the heart. "For out of the heart come evil thoughts, murder, adultery, fornication, theft, false witness, slander. These are what defile a man [before God]" (vv. 19–20 RSV). We notice here two things. (1) The demands of the Decalogue are maintained, but they are concentrated on the demand for a pure heart (cf. 5:17–48). (2) All regulations concerning external (ritual) purity are rendered meaningless. Not a syllable suggests any need to uphold the rules of ritual purity found in the law of Moses. "God's will" is here interpreted in a way which means that a number of concrete commands in the law simply lose their basis. It need hardly be said that such commands are certain to be abandoned in the course of time by those whose zeal is directed toward the purity of the heart and that alone. We know too that the development within the mainstream of Jewish Christianity proceeded in that direction.

Both in the pericope in which Jesus eats with sinners (9:9–13) and in the tradition about the disciples' work on the Sabbath (12:1–8), the prophetic word "I desire mercy, and not sacrifice" (Hos. 6:6) is cited. In its Greek form, this saying is an unambiguous dismissal of sacrifice. Where Hebrew and Aramaic were spoken, however, these words were understood not as abolishing sacrifice but as indicating that deeds of mercy must be given priority over sacrifice. As long as early Christianity retained effective contact with the milieu of its origins, this interpretation was the natural one. But in time the Greek wording had its effect. Especially after the fall of the temple, it was natural to read the text as saying, God is not at all interested in such things as external sacrifices, sacrifices on the temple altar. It is difficult to say how far this development had gone at the time of the evangelist. In the long run it was impossible to stop.

The examples mentioned show what is meant when it is said that Jesus does not abolish the law but fulfills it. He does not formally abolish the concrete demands, but he does effectively minimize their importance. He understands God's demands on humanity as a single, comprehensive demand: that God's children love God and human beings with their whole heart, with all that they are and have. At the core of this "vision" is the conviction that the literal understanding of the concrete commands is much too imperfect an indication of what is required. When the individual commands are examined from the perspective of the fundamental demand on which the divine law is based, it becomes apparent that certain commands must be *radicalized*: this applies to the great ethical commands, especially those enjoining concern for one's fellow human beings. Other commands must be *downplayed*: this applies to commands concerned with ritual and rite, commands which can be fulfilled though the heart does not love God, and which prove rather a hindrance than a help for showing concern to other men. The juridical principle which the Matthean Jesus has urged and pursued with a radicalism which the "scribes and Pharisees" lacked the authority to enforce (7:29) is the principle that lesser commands must give way to weightier. When this principle is pursued radically, the "giving way" tends to become permanent. The lesser commands soon become obsolete. Jesus has applied it so radically that many lesser commands have simply lost their meaning.

The view that this radicalization of the law's central commands is *solely* the result of the impending eschatological crisis seems to me to lack sufficient warrant.

LOVE FOR GOD

In Matthew's version of the pericope concerning the "greatest command" (22:34–40), it is explicitly said that the command to love God (Deut. 6:5) is the "great and first" commandment in the law. This pericope, however, is a relatively late addition to the Matthean tradition adopted from Mark. Evidence for this is, among other things, the fact that the third member of the list is "mind" rather than "strength." Mark's version (12:28–34) has "with (here *ek*) your whole heart and your whole soul and your whole mind (*dianoia*) and your whole strength (*ischys*)." Matthew, in reworking the material, has changed the preposition (from *ek* to *en*) and has omitted the fourth element ("strength"). He has thereby left out the explicit reference to "external resources, power, mammon" but has compensated for this by preserving the important emphasis on "mind." "Insight" plays an important role in Matthew; in addition, "mind" is here undoubtedly meant as that which determines one's attitude toward external resources. Of the command to love one's neighbor (Lev. 19:18), it is said, "A second is like it." This formulation, while not simply reducing the two commands to one, does show that they belong together. The command to love God is a dominant factor in the older Matthean traditions, though the third element there, as in the classical Hebrew version of the *Shema*, is "strength" (interpreted as *mamon*).

The idea that love for God is the most important of all the demands placed on human beings governs most of what is said in the Gospel of Matthew. At times one gets the impression that what God demands is exclusively concern for fellow humans, and that the demand for a positive relationship to the heavenly Father is among those things which may be allowed to fall away (7:12; 19:16–20; 25:31–46); this, however, is—as we shall see later in more detail—directly contrary to the basic thought and main argument of the Gospel. An important premise of the Gospel is that there is only one source for life and life's norms: "One there is who is good" (19:17 RSV); "you have one Father" (23:9 RSV). To be rightly related to him is essential: to love God (22:37); to be a child of the heavenly Father (that is, be like him, 5:45); to do the will of the heavenly Father (7:21; 12:50); to live not by bread alone but by everything which proceeds from the mouth of God (4:4); to hear, understand, and do God's word (13:23).

Absolutely basic is the thought that the children of God's reign must love God *with their whole heart*. This is maintained throughout the Gospel. I would point especially to what has been said above about 13:23; 5:17–48; and 15:1–20. It is because Jesus so strongly demands wholehearted devotion that he so sharply denounces hypocrisy (*hypokrisis*), that is, law observance which has become a mere routine; a pious front (for example, 23:27–28; 7:15–20); pious but empty words (7:21–23; 12:33–37; 15:7–9; 21:28–32); pious but all too facile observance (15:1–9; 23:2–32). The criticism takes many forms, but common to them all is the insistence on wholehearted obedience and love: the "heart" is to be filled and to overflow with love (cf. 12:34–35); then one's attitude toward both God and human beings will be living, genuine, and proper.

The demand that love for God be a love "with your whole soul" finds expression in the parable interpretation in 13:21 and is developed clearly in two texts in particular: 16:21–28 and 10:16–39. The most important saying of Jesus on this theme is the logion "Whoever would save his life [literally, "his soul"—*scilicet*, when God asks him to sacrifice it in martyrdom] will lose it, and whoever loses his life for my sake will find it" (16:25 RSV; cf. 10:39). These words do not express contempt for life. On the contrary, life is regarded as humanity's dearest earthly possession. But the fundamental demands of the divine law are so radical that they do not stop even at life itself; God has the right to require that human beings sacrifice even their lives. God's children are not to reserve anything for themselves when the Father asks them to sacrifice. That good, that truth for which Jesus and his disciples stand is something for which they must also be prepared to die. "If any man would come after me, let him deny himself and take up his cross and follow me" (16:24 RSV). The expression "deny himself" is parallel in meaning to the expression "deny his soul (life)." What is meant is that one says no to the natural will to live and abandons oneself to death. We have in the story of Jesus' passion a concrete example of what this means. There Jesus *confesses* and gives up his life (soul), while Peter in a marked contrast *denies* and thus saves his life (note the deliberate contrast between Jesus and Peter in 16:21–28 and 26:57–75).

The demand that love for God be a love "with your whole strength" in the sense of "external resources, power, mammon" also finds expression in the parable interpretation in chapter 13 (v. 22) and is developed in more detail elsewhere in the Gospel, primarily in 6:24 and 19:16–30. The most important saying of Jesus on this theme is the logion "You cannot serve God and mammon" (6:24 RSV). This logion, which is clearly based on the command to love God in Deut. 6:4–5, says that God demands a love so complete and a service so undivided that no other "master" may be given a share. In the pericope on the rich young man (19:16–26), the evangelist provides an example of a man who does not love God with all his strength (*mamon*). Here we find yet another important logion on this theme: "It is easier for a camel to go through the eye of a needle than for a rich man to enter the kingdom of God" (RSV). Note the wording: difficult, but not impossible (vv. 23–26). In the figure of Judas, Matthew sees an example of how irrevocably the love of mammon can drive love for God even from the heart of a disciple (26:14–16). The other eleven, by way of contrast, are portrayed as exemplary in this respect; they have left all their possessions and followed Jesus (19:27–30; cf. 4:18–22). The negative part of this theme includes not only warnings for the perils of riches but also warnings against the pursuit of power and honor in the eyes of men, "status" (6:1–6, 16–21; 23:2–12, 25–28; and elsewhere).

The ideal attitude is to seek the "promotion" which can only be won by humbling oneself here on earth (20:20–28; 23:11–12; 18:1–5), and to gather "treasure in heaven," heavenly reward (6:1–21; cf. 5:12; 20:1–16).

Thus we see the total picture: in accordance with the fundamental commandment of love for God (Deut. 6:4–5), God's children—the citizens of heaven's kingdom—are to be obedient to the divine word with hearts open and undivided. They are not to go back on the demands God makes, even to save their lives. They are not to forget that the demands of God must determine their attitude toward power and possessions as well.

LOVE FOR ONE'S NEIGHBOR

On this understanding of the command to love God, obeying him continually brings consequences beneficial to one's neighbor. A genuine fulfilling of God's will means a genuine concern for one's fellow human beings—in profound agreement with Lev. 19:18. Note too that others are not here benefited simply by a series of prescribed *deeds*. The "heart" has been opened for positive fellowship, for love and care.

We may point again to 15:1–20: the "purity," the holiness which God desires of a person, is not a matter of external observances designed merely to raise barriers between clean and unclean. It is rather a purity of the "heart," a purity which is for the good of others. Proscribed here are "evil thoughts, murder, adultery, fornication, theft, false witness, slander" (RSV): words and deeds which damage others. In 5:17–48 too we see how "overflowing" obedience toward God comes to expression in a sacrificial, generous attitude toward one's fellows: by not getting angry with one's brother, not violating marriage even in one's heart, not using oaths and asseverations to one's own advantage, but instead doing good in return for evil and embracing even one's enemies and persecutors with love and prayer. When one loves God with one's whole heart (Deut. 6:4–5), people are beneficiaries.

The demand that one be prepared to make sacrifices fits into the same picture. Those who love God with their "whole souls" are ready to endure privation and suffering, even to risk their lives in order to uphold and fulfill the will of a loving God. They are able to share in God's redeeming work even if it costs them their lives (10:5–39). The rich "fruit" borne when life is sacrificed is stressed in a number of Matthean texts, such as the saying about salt (which must disappear into the sacrificial meat in order to have its effect, 5:13), the parable of the mustard seed (which must be buried in the earth if new, abundant life is to be created, 13:31–32; cf. John 12:24), and the parable of the leaven (which must "die" in the dough if all is to be leavened, 13:33). When one loves God with one's whole soul (Deut. 6:4–5), people are beneficiaries.

When love for God determines one's attitude toward property, wealth, and power, there are similar effects. Those who love God with their whole strength are not like those caricatured as devouring "widows' houses" while they "for a pretense make long prayers" (23:14), and who are "full of extortion and rapacity" within (23:25). Those who love God do not promote themselves at the cost of others, nor are they governed by a lust for glory and "status" in the eyes of human beings (6:1–6, 16–21; 23:2–12). They share what they have with others, they part with what they possess for God's sake; should God demand that they abandon all they own, they do it (19:16–30). They do not shrink from being thought "a companion of tax collectors and sinners" (11:19 RSV). When one loves God "with one's whole strength," people are beneficiaries.

It is natural and characteristic for Matthew to speak of God as "the heavenly Father" or "the Father in heaven." (There are twenty occurrences in Matthew, but only one debatable reference in Mark and one borderline case in Luke.) Evidently the general view behind the Gospel is that the children of God are to share in the heavenly Father's familial responsibilities; Jesus' brother, sister, or mother is "whoever does the will of my Father in heaven" (12:46–50 RSV). The two commandments of love for God and love for one's neighbor are kept together. The statement that the latter command is "like" the former (Matt. 22:39) may even be a *technical* indication that each of the two commands is to be interpreted in the other's light, the meaning of each illuminating that of the other (an interpretative principle called g^ezerah shawah, "similar statement," "similar category"). In any case, the thought seems always to be that love for God necessarily expresses itself in love for one's fellow human beings.

According to Matthew, Jesus said of the golden rule, "This is the law and the prophets"; that is, this is what the sacred Scriptures in the final analysis are all about (7:12). This rule is scarcely given its intended force if it is lifted from its context and used as an independent, complete statement of the ethical duty of humankind. In Matthew, it serves as a maximlike pointer expressing in a "popularized" form what is intended by *God's* law and *God's* prophets with all their commands. Still, it is typical that it comes in the midst of teaching where God's will is not presented as a series of rules about holiness and purity, but as markedly ethical, a matter of the heart and of love. Those who are given the task in life not of memorizing and practicing prescribed rules but of taking care of their brothers and sisters are compelled to ask themselves what kind of duties they really have. The golden rule serves then as an easily manageable inner criterion. Those who know what they themselves desire of their fellows in the different situations of life do not have to stand and puzzle in the presence of someone needing their help (cf. the logion in Luke 12:57).

In the pericope of the rich young man, too, we see how the two love commandments are kept together (19:16–26). In answer to the question, what deeds must be done to win eternal life, only the commands of the "second tablet" are mentioned, those dealing with duties toward one's neighbor. But in the introduction (vv. 16–17), we see that Jesus begins by pointing to the One who alone can say what is good and bestow eternal life: "Why do you ask *me* about what is good? *One* there is who is good!" (RSV, emphasis added). Here too duties toward one's neighbor are taken as *God's* commands. And the fundamental statement "The Lord is *one!*" (Deut. 6:4 RSV, emphasis added) is maintained.

The most pointed example of how love for one's fellow human beings is seen as a complete fulfilling of God's will is found in the text dealing with the Last Judgment in 25:31–46. Elsewhere too in the Gospel it is said that the Son of man will judge according to a person's works. Neither what one has claimed to be nor what one appears to be in the eyes of others will be decisive on that day. The heavenly Judge will approve only the one who has obeyed him in heart and in deed, who has *done* his will (7:21–23; 16:27). When the judgment is pictured in detail in 25:31–46, we note that it is *deeds* that are demanded. Furthermore, the deeds mentioned are all of a particular kind. Not one of them is a "work of the law," a prescribed activity done simply because God has commanded it, or in order to maintain the distinction between the people of God and the heathen. Nothing suggesting prescribed observances is mentioned. The deeds here listed belong to a specific category, what were called "acts of mercy" (Hebrew *g^emilut ch^asadim*). This was a traditional category (cf. already Isa. 58:6-7): deeds which show that one has a heart warm to one's fellows—above all, those in need, for whom God has a special responsibility (cf. chapter 2 above). Acts of mercy are thus particularly well suited to disclosing the nature of a person's heart.

The principle of judgment followed is the one we find in 7:2: "measure for measure." The merciful are judged with the divine "measure of mercy" (cf. 5:7). The unmerciful are judged with the "measure of [strict] judgment." Mercy shown to the needy is counted a service done for God in the Old Testament; here it is a "service" done for the Son of man (note 25:44). It is not clear whether the merciful are simply thought to be "credited" with a love for the Son of man or whether they are thought to express an actual (though concealed) love for him (and thus for God). In any case, this text is one of the best examples of how the two love commandments are kept together: if the "second" is fulfilled, the "first" is considered to be fulfilled as well.

This text is part of the material peculiar to Matthew; it is clearly and skillfully formulated. It is undoubtedly a great misuse to take it from its context and interpret it as envisioning a secularized social ethic which is thus commended even by the Gospel. First of all we must bear in mind that the evangelist is not thinking of isolated deeds of charity done now and then by "the righteous" with a reluctant heart because they have been shamed into so doing, or with a desire to be esteemed among people as the motivation. Were that the case, the pericope would conflict with everything else that is said about the attitude God approves. The deeds mentioned are certainly thought of as *typical*; those who do them have the kind of *attitude* which leads them to feed the hungry, and so on. And the one who puts the deeds to the test is the Judge who cannot be deceived by a *superficial* fulfilling of obligations; with eyes of fire he examines heart and action. Moreover, the narrative is certainly not directed to "the last" in order to give them a sense of security in the face of the approaching judgment. It is addressed to "the first" in order to rouse them from the security of their routine, from the confidence they place in creeds or special spiritual gifts or other sources of consolation. Just as in 7:21–23, in the text of the Last Judgment it is stressed that what is decisive is whether or not one has done "the heavenly Father's will." And just as in 19:30 and 20:16, those who are considered "the first" are warned that they may prove to be "the last."

Still, we are left with an incontestable and astonishing fact: genuine, active mercy toward people is candidly portrayed as the fulfillment of the heavenly Father's will. Here the bounds of the Jewish theocracy have been broken through decisively; the detailed sacral regulation of all of life's situations has lost its interest. Attention is centered on sound and adequate concern for people needing help. Some interpreters are inclined to see in the label "the least of these my brothers" a name for Christians. It would thus be deeds done for Jesus' followers which would be the exclusive base for salvation (the logion in 10:42 is usually cited as a parallel). An advanced group egoism of this kind, however, is directly contrary to Jesus' ethic as Matthew interprets it. The judgment of the Son of man shows, according to Matthew, no respect of persons. (Compare what Paul says in Romans 2, a superb commentary on the theme of Matthew 25!) Matthew does indicate that Jesus' earthly ministry was kept within Israel (15:24; 10:5–6), but this restriction is shattered when Jesus' work is complete: then what he has achieved is to be spread to all nations (28:18–20). And the judgment will not take place until the gospel has been proclaimed for all nations (24:13). With this perspective, it cannot have been the evangelist's—or Jesus'—intention that deeds of mercy for the *benefit* of Christians should be the really significant factor in the eyes of the Judge.

We do, however, recognize one feature characteristic of Jesus as Matthew portrays him: he assesses people without reference to the conventions of his time. By not demanding perfect observance of prescribed practices but concentrating instead on the heart's faith and love, Jesus can severely criticize the dominant religious leaders of the people of God—the Pharisees and scribes (chapters 6, 15,

23)—but see repentance and faith in tax collectors and prostitutes (21:31–32), a heathen woman (15:21–28), or an officer in the heathen forces of occupation (8:5–13); indeed, he finds in the latter greater faith than he has encountered in anyone in Israel. Consistent with this is the fact that Jesus can present a child as model for those who want to enter God's kingdom (18:1–5), stress that "babes" grasp more of his teaching than "the wise and understanding" (11: 25–31), and foretell that on the day of judgment many of the "first" shall be "last," and vice versa (19:30; 20:16). As Jesus understands "the heavenly Father's will," one's rank before God will not be determined by age, advanced studies, or accumulated observances of the commandments. Obedience to God is understood in such a way that the child, the unlearned, the immature, even the outsider has a chance to be judged "without respect of persons"; even the "last" can be approved if, in heart and deed, they have done what the heavenly Judge desires to have done. In the passage dealing with the final judgment, the cherished statement "All Israelites have a share in the world to come" is denied. No one, according to the Matthean text, will be saved at the judgment simply by belonging formally to the people of God and fulfilling the trivial external demands put by the law of the theocracy. Not even gifts of prophecy and healing bring acquittal, according to a related text (7:21–23). Nor will any be condemned because they are foreigners, uncircumcised, or ignorant of Sabbath observance and prescriptions of ritual holiness and purity. When the divine demand is seen to require a consistent attitude of openness and love toward God and fellow humanity, then the latent universalism in the old Jewish faith has come to the fore. Once covered by the sacral network which hard times forced the leaders of God's people to develop, it has now been allowed to appear with all its glory. Where the laws of the theocracy prevailed, the individual duties of the children of God have now been brought to light. Moreover, the heavenly Father—he who is "good to all, and his compassion is over all that he has made" (Ps. 145:9 RSV)—has here been interpreted in such a way that *every* thinking person must perceive that the divine demands are proper and inescapable, and that no one has any excuse for hardening one's heart against them. Judgment strikes the "first" especially hard: those who have heard both much and long.

"Many will come from east and west and sit at table with Abraham, Isaac, and Jacob in the kingdom of heaven, while the sons of the reign will be thrown into the outer darkness" (8:11–12).

In the passage on the final judgment we see as well the truly sublime idea of reward found in Matthew's Gospel. It is *unrewarded* deeds of mercy which are rewarded by the blessedness of the reign of heaven. Matthew shares the axiomatic assurance of the rabbis that the Lord of righteousness can never go into debt by allowing people's good and proper deeds to be done in vain, by allowing a faultless "sacrifice" to be offered without being "rewarded." When the matter is viewed so, it becomes important not to constantly demand a return here on earth for one's good works; otherwise one cashes in one's reward already here and now, or even destroys it (6:1–6, 16–18; 10:42). In Matthew's Gospel it is strongly emphasized that "overflowing" deeds of righteousness and those good works not recognized (perhaps not even observed) here on earth will be "rewarded" in the reign of heaven. This faith in a righteous and good Master in heaven provides a special motivation for the desire to make sacrifices which benefit those who either cannot or will not reward one here on earth: those with no strength or resources or significance, as well as outsiders, enemies, and persecutors (note 5:17–48; 6:1–4; 10:41–42; 25:34–40). The reward motif is not, however, given so prominent a place that the primary impulse for action, the heart's genuine love, is imperiled. And one parable deals with the right of the Master in heaven to give a full reward— if he so chooses—to those who have repented so late that, humanly speaking, they have not at all had time to earn it (20:1–16).

JESUS AS MODEL

The ethos which the Matthean Jesus presents to the people of God is, in the evangelist's view, to be realized in the "following" of Christ. When the rich young man points out that he has kept all the commandments—meaning that he has kept them in the traditional, literal sense in which they were understood—he is told that if he wants to be perfect (*teleios*), he must give up all his possessions (mammon) for the good of the poor, then come and follow Jesus (19:16–22). In many other texts as well we see how the love which is wholehearted, ready for martyrdom, all-sacrificing is portrayed as a life spent "following" Jesus or lived "for Jesus' sake" (5:10–12; 10:16–42; 16:24–26; 19:27–30; 20:25–28; and so forth).

In spite of the fact that Jesus is soon to receive all power in heaven and earth, he is by no means himself exalted above the demands he makes of others. On the contrary, it is he who first of all must fulfill them (20:28). It is a capital misunderstanding of Matthew's message to see Jesus as raised above all demands, enjoying divine freedom, appearing to Israel only for purposes of revelation, saying his words and doing what he does only in order to be a pattern for *others* and to teach *them* the right way to live. For Matthew, it is a general law of the kingdom of heaven that no one may enter it who does not do the will of the heavenly Father (7:21–23). This applies even to Jesus. In the full sense of the phrase, *he* must give proof of his "overflowing" love for the heavenly Father. If he does not meet the standard as God's Son, the throne of heaven's reign must await another occupant. Matthew is in fact extremely anxious to show that Jesus in all respects does meet the standard, that he really *does* show love for the heavenly Father in all he is and does, that he actually *does* spend himself in merciful concern for those with whom he comes in contact. Here we must devote a couple of pages to Matthew's portrayal of Jesus from one particular perspective—as fulfiller of the heavenly Father's will.

In the introductory chapters we see that Matthew regards Jesus as the "Son of God" in a different sense than other sons of God; he has no human father but is conceived by divine Spirit (1:18–25). This does not, however, prevent him from being portrayed as the model for all other children of God (citizens of God's reign). How does Matthew depict Jesus' exemplary attitude and work?

Jesus' public ministry is linked with John the Baptist's message of the nearness of heaven's reign (3:2) and of "the way of righteousness" (21:32); and it begins with his baptism and temptation. The baptism and temptation narratives (3:13—4:11) form a kind of prologue to the depiction of Jesus' public activity among the people of God.

At his baptism Jesus receives the Spirit, and heaven confirms that he is God's Son, loved (chosen) by God: "This is my Son, the beloved . . ." The temptation or, better, testing to which he then is exposed will show if he really is God's Son; that is, if he loves his heavenly Father as the Son of God should. How is this testing of the genuineness and perfection of the divine Son portrayed? Naturally enough, it is portrayed as an examination which will show whether he loves his Father with his whole heart, his whole soul, and his whole strength (*mamon*)—just as the fundamental command of the law (Deut. 6:4–5) requires. Thus the testing is threefold.

1. Jesus is first led into a situation of tormenting hunger. (The desires which divided the "heart" before God were, according to the Jewish interpreters, primarily the animal instincts of hunger, thirst, sexual desire, and so forth.) The tempter tries to induce him to give way because of hunger, to abandon his trust in the Father's provision and assume responsibility for procuring his own food (like Israel in the wilderness). But Jesus dismisses the temptation with the words that humankind is primarily to live on that which proceeds from the mouth of God, that a person's heart is thus not to be divided because of animal instincts.

2. Jesus is then urged to cast himself from the "pinnacle of the temple," thus forcing God to intervene miraculously and save him when his life is endangered. But Jesus dismisses this temptation with the words that one is not to tempt God; that is, in this case, to *demand* that God preserve one's life ("soul") from death.

3. Finally, Jesus is offered all the world's mammon—all its power and riches—if he will but fall down to Satan; that is, fall away from the one true God and lapse into idolatry. This temptation Jesus dismisses with the words that God alone is to be worshipped and served.

Thus in the temptation narrative we have a penetrating analysis of the secret of Jesus' relationship with the heavenly Father. Here it is maintained that his genuineness and legitimacy as God's Son lie in the proper, perfect, "overflowing" love he shows for God: the love of heart, soul, and "strength." In this introductory midrashic text, however, the testing is on a theoretical plane. The narrative shows that Jesus has "heard" and "understood" what God demands, and that he is ready to "do" God's will. (As the above discussion shows, the narrator has taken the structure and criteria of the testing from the *Shema*, and from the parable of the sower.)

The portrayal of Jesus' public ministry among the people of God is strongly stylized. His work takes place in two periods. During the first, he stands under God's "blessing" and is active in strength (superiority). During the second he is under the "curse" and is active in weakness (inferiority). He can thus be depicted as the pattern both for "the strong" and for "the weak."

Jesus' activity in strength has two elements closely connected to each other. His main tasks, according to the summarizing editorial notes, are two: (1) to teach and preach the gospel of the reign of heaven, and (2) to heal the sick and drive out evil spirits (4:23; 9:35). His ministry is said to be impelled by mercy (verb: *splanchnizein*, 9:36; cf. 14:14; 15:32; 20:34). Repeatedly Jesus is said to intervene in response to a prayer for mercy (verb: *eleein*, 9:27; 15:22, 17:15; 20:30–31).

Jesus' activity in strength thus expresses itself in (extraordinary) *deeds of mercy*. He appears with incomparable power and authority (*exousia*, 7:29), demonstrates incomparable wisdom (*sophia*, 12:42) and unmatched powers (*dynameis*, 9:33; 11:20–23), thus arousing astonishment and surprise (13:54 and elsewhere). When he teaches, he does not resemble the many who supplement the legal system of the theocracy (7:28–29); his instruction imparts an easy yoke and a light burden to those who can receive it (11:25–30). When he performs his mighty works, the prophetic words of a messianic future must be invoked as a mysterious explanation (11:2–6, citing Isaiah). His whole activity is said to be done because the Spirit of God rests on him (12:15–32). Yet in spite of his unique character, he passes (proleptically) his two main tasks on to the apostles and thus to the church (9:35—10:15), and is clearly depicted as a model.

As "the strong one," then, Jesus accepts the weak and bears their burdens (to use Pauline expressions). His concern is not confined to his attitude and words but includes action for the benefit of those who are tormented in various ways and suffer privation. Their need is expressed in cries to him, cries to which he responds by intervening and sharing of his "riches," both of his incomparable wisdom and of his incomparable power to heal and satisfy. We see here a particular outlook on life and a particular view of humanity. According to Matthew, Jesus takes physical and "material" needs seriously. He heals and feeds and shows concern for the poor. On the other hand, he regards humankind's greatest need as *spiritual*: people's deepest hunger is their hunger for God; their most serious sickness is spiritual obduracy and blindness.

From the very birth of Jesus, the threat of death hangs over his head. During his period of strength, however, he enjoys heavenly protection. He has no difficulty in escaping perilous attacks (2:14, 22; 4:12; 12:14–15; 14:13; 15:21). It is when the "hour" determined by God has come that the situation first changes: blessing is turned to curse, strength to weakness. Protection is withdrawn from him. The heavenly Father delivers him into the hands of his foes, and to a violent death. The turning point is given in 16:21: "From that time Jesus began to show his disciples that he must go to Jerusalem and suffer many things . . ." (RSV). In 16:21–28 we have a description of the attitude which he—and his followers—must take when the heavenly Father requires them to sacrifice their lives for his sake.

At the introduction to the portrayal of Jesus' period of weakness stands the Gethsemane pericope (26:36–46). Here the evangelist shows how Jesus conducts himself, knowing that he is now to be abandoned by God and put to death. He "watches and prays" for his own part, and he admonishes his "brothers." His prayer—certainly understood as exemplary—is a thrice-repeated request that if possible he might be spared from the trial which now threatens. Jesus is not here depicted as a Stoic who regards himself as raised above such things as suffering and death (*apatheia*). Nor is he pictured as one of the many zealous fanatics who embrace death fervently and triumphantly (cf., for example, 2 Macc. 14:37–46). He is portrayed as one who loves life and desires if possible to avoid the violent death ahead, but who still submits to the heavenly Father's will: "nevertheless, not as I will, but as thou wilt" (v. 39 RSV). He is prepared to sacrifice everything, even life itself (his "soul"), in his "overflowing" love for the Father in heaven.

In that which follows, Matthew sees an exemplary attitude under the conditions of the divine "curse": in weakness and suffering. Part of the radical curse and trial is the fact that Jesus is forsaken and abandoned by all who ought to protect and assist him. He is betrayed, not only by the representatives of political authority and the leaders of the people of God, but also by followers and friends;

all support from positive fellowship is withdrawn. How does the evangelist portray Jesus' attitude under these circumstances? His look is not outward, seeking fellowship with the boldness (*parrēsia*) shown by the "strong." He is turned inward, collected and quiet. His few words are necessary words: a brief confession before the Sanhedrin, a single word of confession before Pilate, a single cry of lament and confidence (taken from the sacred Scriptures) on the cross.

The basic thought in the crucifixion narrative is that Jesus gives his "soul" (his life) in a faultless, perfect sacrifice on behalf of "many" (cf. 1:21; 20:28; 26:28). With a number of deliberately chosen formulations, the narrator has intended to show that this sacrifice is perfect, faultless. Jesus sacrifices himself with full *awareness* and with free *will* (note the predictions and the Gethsemane pericope). His sacrifice is thus offered "from the heart," and it is complete. In the details of what happened at Golgotha, the evangelist sees a trial (testing) of the same kind as that found in the temptation narrative, though now it is a literal, desperate reality.

1. 27:33–34. Jesus is deprived of all food and drink: he does not even receive a cup of fresh water to quench his thirst. Just as in the introductory temptation (4:2–4), so now it is required of him that "the evil inclination" of the heart not lead him into rebellion against the will of God.

2. 27:35–37. Jesus is deprived of the last vestiges of power and property. Even the most basic of possessions (the minimum of mammon)—his clothes—are taken from him. And even the most basic power, that of governing his own body and person, has been taken from him; he is nailed fast and guarded. Just as in the introductory temptation (4:8–10), so now it is required of him that he not be so attached to power and property that he is led to rebel against the will of God.

3. 27:38–50. Jesus is deprived of protection and deliverance from violent death. He is put to a death of infamy and disgrace, helped by none and incapable of helping himself. Just as in the introductory temptation (4:5–7), so now it is required of him that he submit to God's will and refuse to demand that God preserve his life from death. Here the crucial point in the testing is reached. The great question is whether Jesus is willing to give up his life (his "soul")

without defiance or disobedience, without complaint or blasphemy, in an "overflow" of obedient love for the Father, who tests him by forsaking and abandoning him.

Jesus stands the test. His sacrifice is made in agreement with the law's fundamental demands (Deut. 6:4–5) and is thus an irreproachable, perfect sacrifice.

THE SITUATION OF THE CHURCH

For Matthew, Jesus is primarily "God's Son." He shows his genuineness as "God's Son" by being "God's servant" with his whole heart, his whole soul, and his whole strength (note 3:17 and 20:28). As a reward for showing this perfect, obedient love and for humbling himself under the will of the heavenly Father even to the point of dying in ignominy, he is exalted and receives power and authority over "heaven and earth" (28:18). He is thereby able to carry out heaven's "policies" according to the guiding principles he outlined during his earthly ministry (28:20a). Matthew does view some things from a salvation-history perspective. "The law and the prophets" have prophesied until the time of John the Baptist. But with him—the "Elijah" of prophecy—a new era begins (11:13–14). Jesus' work on earth is guided by the Spirit (12:15–32) and follows patterns laid down in such prophecies as that of the "servant" (Isaiah 42 and 53) and the "new covenant" (Jeremiah 31). Still, his work reaches its climax first when, after enduring great suffering, he is exalted to "the right hand of Power" (26:64; 28:18–20).

The disciples and, through them, the church are given the commission to continue his work (28:18–20). By baptism and instruction they are to make disciples of all nations. The instruction is to contain "all that I have commanded you" (RSV), a reference to the complete Jesus tradition and thereby also to its background and basis, "the law and the prophets," which Jesus fulfilled rather than abolished (5:17–48 and elsewhere). At the center of the renewed fellowship of God's children is the sacred meal where Jesus' sacrificial work effectively fulfills its function in forgiving sins and creating love (26:26–29). According to Matthew, Jesus, during his earthly ministry, has also provided certain guidelines for the organization of this fellowship (chapters 10; 18; 23; and elsewhere). The presence of the heavenly Lord is promised Jesus' disciples (the church) as they continue his work (28:20; cf. also 18:20).

The attitude which Jesus proclaimed in deed and word—we may call it the "attitude of Christ"—is, as we have seen, one which creates fellowship. It breaks down barriers and establishes fellowship. But it does bring about *one* type of division: it draws upon itself an intensive hatred from those who refuse to accept it (5:10–13; 10:16–42; 16:24–28; 24:9–13; and so forth). Nor does the hatred come exclusively from the heathen; it comes as well from those claiming to be the people of God. Early Christianity has taken up a soul-searching idea earlier formulated by Jewish sages of a sterner sort: God's prophets are always put to death by God's people. This thought plays an important role in the Gospel of Matthew (for example, 5:10–13; 23:29–38). When the Son is killed, it is the natural sequel to the persecution of the prophets (21:33–46); the threat of martyrdom later hangs over Jesus' followers as well (10:24–39; 16:24–26). Here early Christianity has seen a profound mystery: true obedience of the God who is good is not witnessed dispassionately by those who only formally and superficially are counted his children. Routinization of the religious and ethical life comes to expression not only in thoughtlessness and weakness but also as a *defense* against God's true and living demands. Indeed, behind a fanatic zeal for God there may lie obduracy and hatred. An intense ethical program may be pursued at the same time as the heart is hardened and rebellious.

Matthew says little about the Spirit. In his ethical argumentation there is scarcely a reference to the Spirit (cf., however, 10:19–20). Still, the Spirit is a part of his total perspective. Jesus' whole accomplishment is, according to Matthew, impelled by the Spirit (1:18–25; 3:13—4:1; 12:15–32; and so forth). The Spirit, though not mentioned, is presumably thought to play a role when Jesus is pictured as sowing in people's hearts (13:1–23) and revealing how the will of God is to fill and govern people from within their hearts (5:17–48 and elsewhere), but this is not said explicitly. The value Matthew places on Jesus' words is apparent in the sayings about how Jesus with them fulfills "the law and the prophets" (ibid.), and how they must therefore be received and followed (7:24–27; 28:20); indeed, they are eternal and indestructible (24:35).

Matthew is here thinking also in terms of the church. His vision is that the receptive from every nation become by baptism (which, significantly, takes place "in the name of the Father and of the Son and of the Holy Spirit") a part of a holy fellowship—a fellowship marked by submission and obedience to Jesus' words about the divine reign, cost what it may. In this fellowship the heavenly Lord himself is present (18:20; 28:20). Evidently the Spirit is here regarded as "Christ's presence."

And as a memento for Christians who may feel they satisfy all requirements, Matthew has depicted how all of Jesus' followers, including the foremost leaders of the church, with Peter—"the Rock"—at their head, failed Jesus in the moment of cosmic crisis, when the Chosen One himself was put to the decisive test. Undoubtedly Matthew has meant to give his readers a searching reminder that *everyone*—even the church—must in the final analysis fall back on the perfect work of obedient love which Jesus Christ had to perform completely alone when the new covenant was to be established.

BIBLIOGRAPHICAL NOTE

The basis for my interpretation of Matthew's ethos has been developed in the following special studies: *The Testing of God's Son (Matt. 4:1–11 & Par.): An Analysis of an Early Christian Midrash*, part 1 (Lund: C. W. K. Gleerup, 1966); "The Parable of the Sower and its Interpretation," in *New Testament Studies* 14 (1967–68): 165–93; "Jésus livré et abandonné d'après la passion selon Saint Matthieu," in *Revue Biblique* 76 (1969): 206–27; "Ur Matteusevangeliet," in *Ur Nya Testamentet*, 2d ed., ed. L. Hartman (Lund: C. W. K. Gleerup, 1972), pp. 108–50, 163–201; "Geistiger Opferdienst nach Matth 6, 1–6, 16–21," in *Neues Testament und Geschichte* (O. Cullmann *Festschrift*) (Zürich: Theologischer Verlag; Tübingen: J. C. B. Mohr, 1972) pp. 69–77; "Du Judéochristianisme à Jésus par le Shema'," in *Judéo-christianisme* (J. Daniélou *Festschrift*) (Paris: Beauchesne, 1972), pp. 23–36; "The Seven Parables in Matthew XIII," in *New Testament Studies* 19 (1972–73): 16–37; "Monoteism och högkristologi i Matteusevangeliet," in *Svensk Exegetisk Arsbok* 37–38 (1972–73): 125–90; "Gottes Sohn als Diener Gottes," in *Studia Theologica* 27 (1973): 73–106; "The Hermeneutic Program in Matt. 22:37–40," in *Jews, Greeks and Christians* (W. D. Davies *Festschrift*) (Leiden: E. J. Brill, 1976), pp. 129–50. The Swedish versions of seven of these articles have been assembled in the volume "*Hör, Israel!*" *Om Jesus och den gamla bekännelsen* (Lund: LiberLäromedel, 1979). References to other current literature on Matthew can be found in these studies as well. See also the bibliography at the close of this book.

4

Early Christianity's Ethos
According to Paul

THE APOSTLE'S PERSONAL BACKGROUND

The great early Christian teacher behind the Gospel of Matthew (he seems, however, not to have been the one responsible for its final redaction) evidently had had an excellent scribal education before his conversion to Jesus Christ. More specifically, he seems to have received his training within the Pharisaic branch bearing the name "the house of Hillel." Somewhat earlier the young Saul/Paul from Tarsus was educated in the same school, at the time when Gamaliel the Elder was the dominant figure. Both Paul and Matthew made use of their training when they came to formulate the difference between their old faith and their new.

In Acts 22:3, the author has Paul introduce himself in the following manner: "I am a Jew, born at Tarsus in Cilicia, but brought up in this city [that is, Jerusalem] at the feet of Gamaliel, educated according to the strict manner of the law of our fathers, being zealous for God as you all are this day . . ." (RSV). In his Letters Paul himself gives hints as to his background which point in a similar direction: he has received a careful upbringing in the ethos of the Jewish theocracy; he has distinguished himself by his fervent and undivided devotion; in the matter of righteousness—that which is acquired by adhering to the law (Torah)—he has by his own admission been faultless; he claims to have advanced in Judaism beyond many of his compatriots, to have been still more devoted than they to the traditions of the fathers (Phil. 3:5–6; Gal. 1:14). Thus with his mother's milk he has imbibed the traditional outlook on life; from early childhood he has been brought up to put the question to every detail of life: what is forbidden, what permitted? What is clean, and what unclean?

When this man now stands before his congregations as an apostle of Jesus Christ, his outlook on life is radically different: "Everything is clean!" "Nothing is unclean!" "All things are lawful!" (Rom. 14:14, 20; 1 Cor. 6:12). He gives expression to words of freedom and exaltation which can scarcely be outbid: "All things are yours, whether . . . the world or life or death or the present or the future, all are yours!" (1 Cor. 3:21–22 RSV, emphasis added). Gone is the sacral network in which he has been raised, which he made his own and learned not only to respect but also to love and to apply enthusiastically to all areas of life. Before him now lies God's created world, pure and free in the sunlight, permitted, accessible. Every statute has vanished.

The miraculous psychical experience which has brought about this radical shift in outlook and triggered this revolution in thought cannot be discussed in the limited space at our disposal. Still, we must outline briefly the salvation-history viewpoint to which Paul gives expression in his Letters, and which shows how he sees the connection between his old life in the ethos of the Jewish theocracy and his new life as a Christian.

THE SALVATION-HISTORY PERSPECTIVE

Like Matthew, Paul thinks in terms of salvation history and shows an unshakable respect for the law of God (Torah). Among his existential axioms is the belief that God's law has a validity which no man can set aside; should God himself choose to alter it, even he must not violate the principles of law in so doing. As we have seen, the ex-Pharisee *Matthew* claimed that Jesus by no means annulled the law but only fulfilled it. In his view, Jesus had followed in a consistent, radical way the principle that weightier demands take precedence over lighter ones; in the process, the actual will of God received so clear a focus that formal demands of the law lost their inherent value and peripheral commands were thrust aside. The ex-Pharisee *Paul* follows a different juridical principle: the law has no validity outside its sphere; above all, it does not apply to the person who has died. O. Linton has shown that the apostle never reasons in so markedly juridical a way as when he comes to explain how there can be freedom from the divine law.

Having come to the insight that Jesus of Nazareth was the Son of God—Lord and Messiah—and that salvation and life are given freely through him and not by means of the law (Torah), Paul has been compelled to ask himself the question, what was the real purpose of the law? (cf. Gal. 3:19). He has settled on two things: (1) The law cannot be eternal. It does not come first, nor does it prevail until the end (Gal. 3:17–29). The task it has to perform applies to one epoch of salvation history. Paul distinguishes the following epochs. First comes the period from Adam until Moses. The Torah does not then exist (Rom. 5:13, 20). On the other hand, the *promise of salvation* is given during this time (Romans 4; Galatians 3). The law is intended for the period which follows: it is given on Sinai, and its period ends with Christ (Rom. 5:20; Gal. 3:19). Since the death and resurrection of Christ, not law but grace prevails (Rom. 5:15; cf. 3:19, 21). (2) The law can never have been intended to save, to give eternal life. During its limited period of validity it has had a limited purpose: to be a "custodian" for the people of God until they come of age (Gal. 3:15—4:7), to uncover sin, bring knowledge of sin, and—paradoxically enough—even provoke and increase sin as a preparation for Christ (Rom. 5:12–21; Gal. 3:10—4:7; cf. Rom. 3:20; 7:7). Thus, in Christ the law (Torah) has reached its end (Rom. 10:4). Here salvation is given—"the righteousness of God"—and it is given *without law*; it is completely free and is to be received by faith (see, for example, Rom. 1:16–17; 3:21–30). A new covenant has been entered (2 Cor. 3:1–18).

Paul's thinking with regard to Gentiles is in part analogous to this. They do not have the Torah, but they do have a certain knowledge of the will of God, clouded though that knowledge is (Romans 1—2). Now they are in bondage to false gods and spiritual powers as well as to laws, statutes, requirements, and commands from cruel masters of different kinds (1 Cor. 12:2; Gal. 4:8; Col. 2:20; and so forth). But they too may now receive freedom in and through Christ. The alternative to what is now offered, for both Jews and Gentiles, is the wrath of God (Rom. 1:18—3:20).

Paul is not, however, thinking in purely temporal terms. He certainly does not mean that all statutes everywhere collapsed and lost their validity when Christ died, so that the world now finds itself in a law-free era. No, "Christ is the end of the law for righteousness *to every one that believeth*" (Rom. 10:4 KJV; cf. 1 Cor. 9:20–21). The freedom from the law which Christ has brought about is only available within the sphere which Paul speaks of as "in Christ." It is "in Christ" that what is old has passed away and a new creation has come into being (2 Cor. 5:17–18). Everything is pure, everything permitted *for those who are "in Christ"* (Rom. 14:14; 1 Cor. 6:12). It is thus crucial that one enter that sphere.

The person who receives circumcision puts himself under the law. He is obligated to keep it as long as he lives (Gal. 5:3). Jesus himself was under the law (Gal. 4:4). But the law does not rule a man after he has died. At death he is free from the law's demands upon him. Law does not apply to the dead (Rom. 7:1; 6:7). For Paul, this juridical principle is axiomatic. When Christ arose from the dead, he was free from the law. Further, his death was a death for all (2 Cor. 5:14–15 and elsewhere). A law-free zone surrounds the resurrected Christ. The one who enters that zone partakes of its freedom. Paul claims that this takes place ritually, by baptism. Baptism is in the eyes of God a valid death, a death with Christ and into Christ (Rom. 6:1–11, and so forth). Those who are baptized into Christ have the right to regard themselves as dead to that world over which the law reigns. They have emigrated to the realm of freedom (Rom. 6:1—7:6; Gal. 2:19–20). They have died, and their "life is hid with Christ in God" (Col. 3:1–3). They enjoy a "post-mortem" freedom.

But for those who have not, by baptism and faith, died with Christ, slavery continues: slavery under Torah and under "the powers of this world," with the wrath of God as their hopeless prospect. At times Paul expresses himself as though he meant that the demands of the law still apply even for those who are "in Christ," and that Christ only created the necessary preconditions for a fulfilling of the law. "The just requirement of the law" is "fulfilled in us, who walk . . . according to the Spirit," he writes in Rom. 8:4. But the apostle's words are not to be understood in that sense. He claims that the one who has died with Christ has radically and completely left the sphere of the law, entering a sphere where the Spirit rules and really creates freedom (2 Cor. 3:17; Gal. 5:18; and so forth). And the law has never exercised any authority over the Spirit, not even during the "period of the law." It has never been entitled to prescribe for the Spirit of God what it may and may not do. What Paul means in texts such as Rom. 8:4 is that the Spirit can never do anything which is wrong in the eyes of God. For that reason it is axiomatic for the apostle that the law—rightly understood—can never have any objection to raise against that which the Spirit does: "against such there is no law," he writes after listing the effects of the Spirit (Gal. 5:22–23).

When one has died to the law and its demands, one is free: free from obligations, but also free from guilt. Where law has no validity, wrongdoing cannot be prosecuted. "Where there is no law there is no transgression" (Rom. 4:15 RSV). The death of the criminal puts an end to the charges against him; charges cannot be pressed against a dead man. "He who has died is freed from sin" (Rom. 6:7 RSV). Using simple juridical principles of this kind, Paul illustrates what it means to have left the sphere of the Torah and entered that of the risen Lord. But what does freedom "in Christ" mean positively?

FREEDOM "IN CHRIST"

With a radicalism and a clarity unparalleled in the other books of the New Testament, Paul presents what the *gospel* is: a completely unconditional offer of all the good at God's disposal. In the gospel "the righteousness of God" is revealed, and that "apart from law"— that is, without the Torah serving as a means; and it is bestowed with royal generosity on each and every person who believes. The whole process begins with God; further, all the hindrances which block the way are removed without any activity on the part of the recipients which might earn the incomparable gift (Rom. 1:16–17; 3:21–26; 2 Cor. 5:14–21; and so forth). What has here especially captured the attention of the apostle—understandably enough—is the fact that the worst "sinners," "heathen" gone desperately astray, can receive something they are far from deserving. "God shows his love for us in that while we were yet sinners Christ died for us" (Rom. 5:8 RSV). Moreover, the demonstration of "God's love in Christ Jesus our Lord" (Rom. 8:39) is not confined to a single intervention in the past; it characterizes God's continual activity in the present as well. Clearly and in countless variations Paul develops the basic thought that God "in Christ" *gives and gives again.*

The relation which God has thus established with his people has, to be sure, been constituted in a legal way (Rom. 3:31), but it is not a relation regulated by laws and statutes. "In Christ," the formulas "without law" and "without the works of the law" apply. Admittedly, Paul finds it natural to regard Christians as citizens in God's kingdom, the kingdom which will appear in visible form when the appointed time has come (Phil. 3:20); but he regards them as free citizens, indeed, children of the king (Rom. 8:14–17; Gal. 4:4–7; and so forth); it is with great reluctance that he uses the word "law" when he describes how they are to conduct themselves. Part of the problem is that the Greek word for "law" (*nomos*) is considerably more rigid in its meaning than its Hebrew counterpart (*torah*); hence it is ill-suited for a description of a life style characterized by radical freedom. The apostle does use the phrase "law of Christ" once, but he does so in a way that suggests his awareness that the expression is not quite adequate: "Bear one another's burdens, and so fulfill the 'law of Christ' " (Gal. 6:2 RSV, quotation marks added). We get the same feeling that Paul is resorting for the moment to language which has its hazards when we read his declaration that he is not "without law" but *ennomos Christou*, "Christ-regulated" (1 Cor. 9:21). Similarly, "the law of the Spirit of life" (RSV) in Rom. 8:2 is an isolated expression not belonging to the apostle's normal language—to the extent that his writings permit an opinion on that.

On the other hand, the former contender for the law does find it natural to speak of *freedom*: freedom from all laws and commandments and statutes. The Pauline Letters teem with strong, crisp expressions of a bold, liberated, exalted zest for life. Nor are expressions of this kind confined to spontaneous, emotional outpourings. His zest for life has inspired a new, well-thought-out, fundamental outlook on life, an outlook which the apostle puts forward with an argumentation which often is strikingly rational.

Thus "in Christ" everything is pure, everything free, everything permitted. This, however, does not mean lordless anarchy, in which everyone does as he pleases (that is, satisfies his selfish desires without taking others into account). Everything is filled by the Spirit, and everything is dependent on the one who is the focal point of those who are free and the source of their life: Christ. Typically, the words "all are yours" which were cited above lead into their necessary complement: "and you are Christ's; and Christ is God's" (1 Cor. 3:23 RSV).

Hence when Paul speaks of Christian freedom, he does not mean any privilege on the part of lordless, isolated individuals to expand in whatever direction their vanity may dictate. Freedom is a state of affairs maintained by the one who is freedom's source: Christ—in his union with God. When the connection with this nerve center is broken, freedom ends. Paul can even describe the Christian's necessary contact with freedom's source paradoxically as a "slavery," namely, a slavery under Christ (1 Cor. 7:22 and elsewhere), but this is deliberately paradoxical. The "slavery" in this case means serving "in the new life of the Spirit" (Rom. 7:6). Still, an important—indeed, indispensable—part of Paul's thinking is the view that Christians are not their own masters. They have been purchased from cruel masters and now belong to Christ (1 Cor. 6:19–20; 7:23; Gal. 3:13–14; and so forth). "In Christ" all enjoy life through their Lord. "None of us lives to himself, and none of us dies to himself. If we live, we live to the Lord, and if we die, we die to the Lord; so then, whether we live or whether we die, we are the Lord's" (Rom. 14:7–8 RSV; cf. Gal. 2:19–20).

Freedom is thus something which is constantly received, just as life is received. But freedom is also constantly threatened. Various powers and lords advance from all directions, intending to subjugate and enslave. Not—as we have seen—that they have any right to do so, but it is part of their nature to do so just the same. Time and time again Paul develops the theme that freedom must be asserted and preserved.

The first threat is that of *sin*. Paul almost always speaks of sin in the singular; it is for him a force, a "power" which has wreaked havoc in the world ever since Adam's fall (cf., for example, Rom. 5:12–21) and which leads to death. But for those who are "in Christ" it is a "foreign" power which no longer has the right to rule them. They have left sin's domain. "He who has died is freed from sin" (Rom. 6:7 RSV). The *compulsion* to sin has thus ended. This is Paul's starting point when he admonishes Christians to guard themselves against the slavery which sin imposes on humanity. "You also must consider yourselves dead to sin and alive to God in Christ Jesus. Let not sin therefore reign in your mortal bodies. . . . Do not

yield your members to sin as instruments of wickedness . . ."
(RSV). The clearest presentation of how Paul thinks on this matter
is found in Romans 6—7.

In these chapters we see as well how the "flesh" is one of those
powers which can put an end to the Christian's freedom. The body,
the "flesh," with its desires, is the most accessible point of attack
sin has in a person. The law provokes human lusts into rebelling
against God's will (Romans 7). These desires struggle against the
Spirit as well (Gal. 5:17), and the "flesh" is a constant threat to
enslave a person. Paul warns against living "according to the flesh"
(for example, Rom. 8:1–17; cf. 2 Cor. 10:1–6), against doing "the
works of the flesh" (Gal. 5:13–21). When he lists typical examples
of these, he shows that he is not thinking of natural sensuality but
of selfishness and unbridled passions. The apostle returns repeatedly
to this theme, the necessity of guarding one's freedom by carrying
on a hard and constant struggle with the "flesh," that is, with "sin
in the flesh." Among his—and early Christianity's—standing exhortations is a series of statements to the effect that one is to "put
off" those sins which are typical of "the old man" and "put on"
instead the free, "new man" which is created in Christ's image
(Rom. 13:11–14; Eph. 4:17–32; Col. 3:5–17; 1 Thess. 5:4–11; and so
forth).

A further threat to enchain Christians and end their freedom is
to be found in the *opinions of human beings*, their judgments, sanctions, and praise as well as their values and conventions (Gal. 1:10;
5:1; Col. 2:16; and so forth). In Paul's statements as to the in-
violability of conscience we see how strongly he is on his guard to
preserve freedom from this kind of slavery. Not even the conscience
of another—to which Paul assigns an extraordinary authority—has
any right to prescribe laws for, or bring judgment against, the
Christian's own conscience. "Why should my liberty be judged by
another man's conscience?" (1 Cor. 10:29; cf. Rom. 14:1–2).

Laws and statutes of different kinds represent another threat.
Gentiles who came to faith often (and quite understandably)
brought with them into the Christian congregation laws, taboos,
and conventions from their pre-Christian days, norms which were
invested with ancient, deep-rooted authority and which claimed
continued obedience. Paul does show concern for those who have

been unable to appropriate freedom "in Christ" emotionally, but he strongly combats the tendency to maintain irrelevant obligations of this kind. Do you want to turn back again to the weak and beggarly "powers" and be their slaves again? he writes with both despair and irony (Gal. 4:8–11; cf. Col. 2:16–23). He sees a still greater peril in the attempt to demand that Gentiles who have become Christians be circumcised. In such an attempt he finds Christ's whole work treated as inadequate, its effects voided. His line of reasoning—which again shows how unshakably binding he regarded the demands of the Torah—is, in brief, as follows. When Christians allow themselves to be circumcised, they put themselves under the law (Torah) and are bound to observe it—and to observe it in its entirety. They thus relinquish the freedom which Christ has won and which they themselves duly acquired when they died in baptism to all statutes and united their lives with Christ (Gal. 5:1–12; 2:11–3:4). Paul warns too against *new* "yokes of slavery," new laws and statutes which limit and destroy freedom "in Christ" (Col. 2:20–23).

Against all such threats, then, Paul asserts and guards Christian freedom. At the same time, however, he sees that certain ways of behaving are necessary and that all Christians ought to recognize this and voluntarily—*with their inner freedom preserved*—adopt them. This brings us to the fact that life "in Christ" means not only freedom but also *service*. The Christ who is the Lord of freedom and who bestows freedom has himself demonstrated that freedom can be used to serve—indeed, that true freedom *is* serving, when serving is correctly understood.

"WALKING IN THE SPIRIT"

Paul does not have the same possibilities as were open to Matthew to describe the Christian's ethos strictly and concretely. For Matthew, the law abides. The problem is to show how the law is to be understood and applied. For Paul, the period of the law is at its end. "In Christ" it does not exist. There a living and proper ethos prevails, against which the law—that is, the law rightly understood—can raise no objections. But the ethos which there takes shape is impelled by the Spirit of life; and just as leaves on a tree always differ, so it is dynamic and diverse. Paul has to employ all the enormous arsenal of verbal expressions at his disposal—indeed, at times he must even throw off the laws under which Greek grammarians labor—when he comes to present the ethos to which the impelling of the Spirit gives birth "in Christ." We will here take up just a few aspects of the apostle's rich description.

One consequence of freedom "in Christ" is that Paul cannot impose laws on his Christian brothers and sisters. Nonetheless he feels both entitled and obligated to instruct and exhort; admonition (*paraenesis*) has now replaced halakha. The admonition in Gal. 5:25 is typical: "If we live by the Spirit, let us also walk by the Spirit" (RSV; cf. 5:16). Thus the Christian life can be depicted as a conscious walking "in the Spirit" or "according to the Spirit" (Rom. 8:4). The expression is virtually synonymous with such formulas as "walk in Christ" (Col. 2:6), "walk in newness of life" (Rom. 6:4 RSV), and "walk in love" (Rom. 14:15 RSV; Eph. 5:2).

What does this mean, concretely? That life "in Christ" is a life in the church's sacramental fellowship with Christ is obvious, but this statement only indicates the framework. The contours become clearer when we turn to the important texts in which the apostle says that Christians are to be renewed in their "I"-center, in their "mind" (*nous*) or "heart" (*kardia*), so that they have the capacity to "prove" (*dokimazein*) or "understand" (*synienai*) what is "the will of God," what is "good and acceptable and perfect" (Rom. 12:2; Eph. 5:10, 17; Phil. 1:9–11), and so forth. That the ethical discernment of a person is thus emphasized is of course part and parcel of the fact that life is no longer governed by external commandments and statutes. But we notice here something else as well. Paul does not regard Christians as leaves borne by the Spirit's wind without wills of their own, or as "possessed" by the Spirit. He regards them as free and responsible; the Spirit impels them from within their own beings' inmost centers. The Christian is a child of God, not a slave in bondage (cf. Galatians 3—4, and elsewhere). Paul stresses that Christians in the eyes of God are *grown-up* children, children come of age (ibid.).

Nonetheless, even free people need help and information, especially if their gifts are limited. Paul is well aware that Christian congregations are by no means made up of perfect spiritual heroes. That is why the apostle teaches, and in doing so, he is eager to set forth an example to be imitated: Jesus Christ himself. (We shall return below to other forms of imitation.) At such times it is the leading, fundamental principle in Jesus' conduct which he wants to illustrate: self-sacrificing love, with heart, soul, and *mamon* (Deut. 6:4–5). The texts show that the apostle wants to impress the following on his readers. Jesus had a heart which could forgive (Col. 3:13). Jesus loved people so greatly that he gave himself up (in death) as a sacrifice (Eph. 5:1–2; cf. 5:25). Jesus did not please himself (Rom. 15:3). Jesus did not seek his own best but that of the many, so that they could be saved (1 Cor. 10:33—11:1). Jesus sacrificed his riches and his glory and "for your sake . . . became poor, so that by his poverty you might become rich" (2 Cor. 8:9 RSV). Most detailed is the hymn in Phil. 2:4–11, in which Jesus is depicted as a model of unbounded obedience to God, obedience "unto death, even death on a cross" (RSV).

When Paul points in these texts to Jesus' example, it is, as was already suggested, the actual fundamental principle in Jesus' conduct which he actualizes: Christ is perfect and has everything— freedom and independence, life, glory, power, and wealth—since he is like God himself; nonetheless he chooses to sacrifice himself and all that is his for the benefit of those he loves. And a perfect sacrifice can never be fruitless: that is one of the most elementary axioms of faith. A perfect sacrifice must provoke a divine response. Thoughts are thus drawn to an exalting, unending prospect, expectations of "what no eye has seen, nor ear heard, nor the heart of man conceived, what God has prepared for those who love him" (1 Cor. 2:9 RSV).

Christ is thus depicted as the one who sacrifices himself. It is not an external sacrifice which he brings to the altar. He performs what Paul—linking up with older formulations about martyrdom which speak of it as a sacrifice of one's own body to God—calls "a spiritual altar-service" (Rom. 12:1). That his sacrifice is greater than others' results from who he is. Christ is thus portrayed as the one who demonstrates perfect "love" (*agapē*). That Paul sees the matter so is easily verified. Not only does he explicitly say that Christ sacrificed himself because of love (especially Eph. 5:2, 25; Gal. 2:20); he also describes Christ as the one who did not "look to his own interests." When Christ is presented as a model in Philippians 2, it is with the following introduction: "Let each of you look not only

73

to his own interests, but also to the interests of others" (v. 4 RSV). Among the characteristics of love is the fact that it does not "seek its own" (1 Cor. 13:5; cf. 1 Cor. 10:24). This principle was, according to the apostle, a guiding one for Jesus. The same thing is expressed in the formulas "not seeking one's own advantage" (1 Cor. 10:33) and "not pleasing oneself" (Rom. 15:1–3). In addition to these definitions of what love is, we meet a variant of the golden rule in Rom. 13:10: "Love does no wrong to a neighbor; therefore love is the fulfilling of the law" (RSV).

We have now touched on two of the methods by which Paul tells his fellow Christians how walking "in the Spirit" is to take form: partly by presenting Christ as the example, partly by describing self-sacrificing love (*agapē*) in various ways. Something more must be said about "love" as the dominant element in Pauline exhortation. Paul can at times treat love as though it were one virtue among others, but it is significant that in such lists love either comes first (as firstling) (Gal. 5:22) or last (as summation) (2 Cor. 6:6). There are many other ways in which love's fundamental, all-encompassing role is expressed. It is said to bind "everything together in perfect harmony" (Col. 3:14 RSV). Everything the Christian does is to be "done in love" (1 Cor. 16:14); Christians are to be "rooted and grounded in love" (Eph. 3:17); love is said to be the genuine "fulfilling of the law" (Rom. 13:8–10; Gal. 5:13–14). In a statement of fundamental import the apostle says that "God's love has been poured into our hearts through the Holy Spirit which has been given to us" (Rom. 5:5). And in the elevated prose of 1 Corinthians 13, all accomplishments—even the greatest—are declared to be wind and vanity if love is not found in the heart. (Incidentally, we also see in 1 Cor. 13:1–3 how well Paul remembers the sophisticated interpretation, learned in his youth from Pharisaic scribes, of the commandment to love God in Deut. 6:4–5.)

It has often been pointed out that when Paul uses the word "love" (*agapē*), he seldom seems to mean love for God. The proper attitude toward God in Pauline terms is "faith" (*pistis*) or "obedience" (*hypakoē*). On the other hand, it is very significant that Paul links faith (in God) with love (for one's neighbor). This is apparent not only from the fact that he tends to let *pistis* and *agapē* form a pair (for example, Gal. 5:6; 1 Thess. 3:6; 2 Thess. 1:3) or, together with *elpis* ("hope"), a triad (1 Cor. 13:13; Col. 1:4–5; 1 Thess. 1:2); it is also evident from the fact that Paul holds fast to the general tenet of Christianity that the Last Judgment will be a judgment according to works. This tenet, which Paul clearly states (Rom. 2:5–13; 14:10–12; 2 Cor. 5:10; Col. 3:24–25), appears to blunt the edge of Paul's teaching about justification by faith. But Paul obviously shares the conviction that a right relation to God necessarily carries with it love for people. The faith which is really alive "works through love" (Gal. 5:6). Hence the final examination can limit itself to being a test of works. By "works" here Paul of course does not mean the superficial compliance with the law which he calls "the works of the law." The law has been removed from the scene. Paul means "good works," deeds done out of love for fellow human beings ("acts of mercy"). He does not really believe that the one who has truly come to faith in Christ might be condemned at the judgment. "There is therefore now no condemnation for those who are in Christ Jesus" (Rom. 8:1 RSV). When he speaks of judgment according to works for Christians, he is undoubtedly referring rather to a more nuanced distribution of "rewards" or "punishments," and not to the simple alternatives of salvation or damnation. But he does of course mean that those who are only *apparently* Christians will be rejected at the judgment and finally condemned— a conviction shared by early Christians everywhere.

We see then that Paul, both when he portrays Christ as the pattern and when he describes what love is, presents a characteristic *attitude for life*: a self-sacrificing, serving attitude, directed toward one's fellows. On the other hand, Paul has nothing positive to say about external commands and sacral rules, "works of the law," prescriptions of ritual purity, the circumcision which is only physical, and the like (for example, Rom. 2:25–29; 1 Cor. 7:19; Gal. 5:6; 6:15). In his view, the life of the Spirit has little to do with things like these.

There is a completeness, a synthesizing force in Paul's total outlook, which we cannot here do justice to but can only remind of. The Christ who is Lord and pattern for all God's children is, according to Paul, the image (*eikōn*, 2 Cor. 4:4; and elsewhere) of God; his attitude shows the right way to use likeness with God (Phil. 2:6). Here, then, a vision of creation unites with one of salvation.

75

Christ represents not only something new but also the pristine, what has everywhere been lost in the world of sin. The transformation which now takes place "in Christ" and which will be complete at the Parousia (2 Cor. 3:18; 1 Cor. 15:20–28, 50–57; and so forth), when God's children will receive their full glory and all creation will be delivered from its bondage (Rom. 8:19–21)—this transformation reflects the lost likeness with God which was humanity's "in the beginning." In Ephesians and Colossians these cosmic perspectives are developed extensively; in the older Pauline Letters they remain brief suggestions.

The completeness of Paul's view of life "in Christ" is apparent too in his conviction that the glorified Lord is present not only in the congregation but also in the individual Christian. The pattern for a new human life which, according to Paul, exists in the heart of every Christian is not one ideal among others; rather, it is the divine Lord himself, present in a mysterious way (Gal. 2:19–21; Eph. 3:14–21; and so forth). The fellowship with Christ in prayer and worship in which Paul lives and to which he exhorts his churches ("Pray constantly!" 1 Thess. 5:17) will not be dealt with here.

We may now return to the theme of freedom "in Christ." This freedom is to be guarded against everything that might enslave. But it is to be exercised in an exalted and free service. The strong are—of their own free will—to serve the weak (Rom. 15:1–3). The free are—voluntarily—to be able to abstain from their rights and limit their possibilities (Romans 14; 1 Corinthians 8—10); indeed, they are to be able to become slaves for the sake of those who might be saved in this way (1 Cor. 9:19; cf. Gal. 5:13). Such is the model Paul himself follows when he imitates Christ (1 Cor. 10:32—11:1).

INNER FREEDOM AND CONTROL

Frequently in the letters of Paul the argument takes on a form which is rhythmic and poetic. Repeatedly his readers are asked to share in a "vision" presented in hymnic form. The Christ hymn in Phil. 2:5–11 and the *agapē* text in 1 Corinthians 13 are well-known instances. But to the same category belong several sections in which Paul depicts his own and his fellow Christians' life in this world, describing their independence from external circumstances: from the political situation, economic conditions, and social relationships. Citizens of the coming kingdom of heaven live with eyes fixed on the resurrection and the eternal life ahead—sustained by their faith in the one who is coming and by their hope for that which is to come, inspired from within by the Spirit and the indwelling Christ, and patterning their lives according to the example given by Jesus' own way of living and acting. Though they are under severe attack from without, they neither alter their course nor permit themselves to adopt their attackers' methods. The sufferings they encounter "for Christ's sake" are interpreted as "afflictions of Christ," "sufferings of Christ" (1 Cor. 4:9–13; 2 Cor. 1:3–7; Col. 1:24–26), and are seen as a natural continuation of what Jesus experienced; "afflictions are to be our lot" (1 Thess. 3:3 and elsewhere). The proper outlook is clear. "As servants of God we commend ourselves in every way: through great endurance, in afflictions, hardships, calamities, beatings, imprisonments, tumults, labors, watching, hunger; by purity, knowledge, forbearance, kindness, the Holy Spirit, genuine love, truthful speech, and the power of God; with the weapons of righteousness for the right hand and for the left; in honor and dishonor, in ill repute and good repute. We are treated as impostors, and yet are true; as unknown, and yet well known; as dying, and behold we live; as punished, and yet not killed; as sorrowful, yet always rejoicing; as poor, yet making many rich; as having nothing, and yet possessing everything" (2 Cor. 6:4–10 RSV). "To the present hour we hunger and thirst, we are ill-clad and buffeted and homeless, and we labor, working with our own hands. When reviled, we bless; when persecuted, we endure; when slandered, we try to conciliate; we have become, and are now, as the refuse of the world, the offscouring of all things" (1 Cor. 4:11–13 RSV). A similar passage is found in 2 Cor. 4:7–18, where it is specially emphasized that this attitude is produced by the Spirit and inspired by the thought of the heavenly kingdom's coming.

Typical of this outlook are its independence and inner control; it is governed from within—because it is governed from heaven. The one who speaks so is liberated and free in his heart; he has control over his lusts and is above needing to take revenge and retaliate. The classical mechanisms which cause one to be formed and steered according to the treatment one meets at the hands of others have here been rendered powerless by a stronger force. The one who speaks in this way can forgive; he can repay in his own currency, which is that of love. Threats of sanctions, persecutions, suffering, and death hold no terror for him, nor can they dictate his behavior; he is prepared for everything. His link with the greatest power in the universe gives him undaunted courage: "If God is for us, who is against us?" (Rom. 8:31–39 and elsewhere). He is free too from dependence on human relations, free from the sly pursuit of "remunerations" from other people; he strives for neither status nor affluence. Like Christ, he can part with what he has, even reduce himself to poverty for the sake of those in need. In another text Paul describes his inner freedom and control in the following way: "Not that I complain of want; for I have learned, in whatever state I am, to be content (*autarkēs*). I know how to be abased, and I know how to abound; in any and all circumstances I have learned the secret of facing plenty and hunger, abundance and want. I can do all things in him who strengthens me" (Phil. 4:11–13 RSV).

Paul, in his inner freedom, is not only liberated and superior in relation to the world. He goes· so far that he—at least at times— seems to have as his ideal to be *detached* from the world. The strong words in 1 Cor. 7:29–31 are well known: "The appointed time has grown very short; from now on, let those who have wives live as though they had none, and those who mourn as though they were not mourning, and those who rejoice as though they were not rejoicing, and those who buy as though they had no goods, and those who deal with the world as though they had no dealings with it. For the form of this world is passing away" (RSV). The ideal here sketched recalls the ethical program of the Stoics. Still, at least two crucial differences are immediately apparent. In Paul's case, this ethical ideal has its motivation in salvation history (eschatology): the present world order is coming to an end, and in the time of agonies ahead it is best to remain free, detached from all ties, and thus able both to endure and to serve the Lord with undivided fervor. Furthermore, in Paul's case the liberation and freedom he speaks of are *received*—in a relationship of personal fellowship with the ultimate source of power—not won by one's own heroic struggle. But as H. Preisker has pointed out, the freedom of which Paul here speaks undoubtedly threatens to loosen the bonds of complete love for one's neighbor; it is significant that the distancing attitude is even to come between husband and wife.

CHRISTIANS AND OTHERS

Paul does not feel called upon to present a universal ethos on which everybody, whether believer or not, will be able to unite. His calling is—as he stresses in his every Letter—to preach the gospel of Jesus Christ as an apostle (see especially 1 Cor. 1:17). The ethos he represents is not the primary theme of his message but simply a consequence of that which comes first and carries the greatest weight: the message of salvation. Further, this ethos is to be realized within the sphere which Paul calls "in Christ." It takes form among those who (by baptism) have died to the conditions which bind the rest of humankind, and who have now arisen, or are soon to rise, "with Christ"—those who share in the freedom and power of the resurrection life. It is a product of the Spirit, who is active within this sphere as a first installment of the powers of the eternal life to come.

How does Paul regard the ethical level and standards of the "heathen"? If we begin with his broad, general perspective, we find the heathen painted in a dark contrast to the people of God. The cause of the moral depravity which Paul ascribes to them is their falling away from God. Because of this, they have been abandoned to the hardness of their hearts, their powers of ethical perception have been dimmed, and their capacity for moral action has been paralyzed (Rom. 1:18–32; cf. Eph. 4:17–19). Now they are in bondage to false gods, dark powers, and cruel statutes (1 Cor. 8:4–6; 12:2; Gal. 4:8–11; Eph. 2:11–12). They are the helpless prey of their desires and lusts (1 Cor. 6:9–11; Col. 3:5–7; 1 Thess. 4:5). They are—to put it another way—"dead" in their sins (Eph. 2:1–3; Col. 2:13–23), and so forth. Nevertheless, even when Paul views the actual condition of the heathen in these dark terms, he never forgets that they have been created by God and that God still has dealings with them.

Those who have come to faith in Christ have been drawn out of darkness into the light. And their standing obligates them to adopt an entirely different life style: "Once you were darkness, but now you are light in the Lord; walk as children of light. . . . Take no part in the unfruitful works of darkness . . ." (Eph. 5:1–20 RSV). Paul exhorts his churches to live up to the name "children of light," to live so that they may be "blameless and innocent, children of God without blemish in the midst of a crooked and perverse generation, among whom you shine as lights in the world" (Phil. 2:15 RSV). Christians are not to be "conformed to this world," but "transformed" by their minds' "renewal" (Rom. 12:1–2). They are not to "walk like heathen" (1 Thess. 4:1–8; Eph. 4:17–24). They are to "lead a life worthy of their calling," "worthy of God" who has called them, "worthy of the Lord," "worthy of the gospel of Christ" (Eph. 4:1; 1 Thess. 2:12; Col. 1:10; Phil. 1:27). They are to behave "as befits the saints" (Rom. 16:2; Eph. 5:3 and elsewhere), and so on. At times Paul goes so far as to prescribe direct isolation from a contaminating heathen milieu such as that in Corinth (2 Cor. 6:14—7:1) and admonishes the church in extreme cases to purify itself by isolating or even expelling patent sinners, whose example might affect others just as leaven spreads in dough (Rom. 16:17; 1 Corinthians 5; 2 Thess. 3:6–15; cf. 1 Tim. 1:20; 2 Tim. 3:1–9; Titus 3:10–11). (He is not, however, as rigorous in matters of church discipline as the authors of the Epistle to the Hebrews and Revelation; cf. Heb. 6:4–8; Rev. 2:6, 14–16, 20.) Traditional motifs—the people of God are "chosen," "holy," "children of light," and so forth—are here used.

Is the view justified that Paul at such times speaks contrary to his own newly acquired central intentions? Perhaps to a certain extent it is. Be that as it may, there is a kind of spiritual "pride of birth" which pervades everything Paul has to say, and he regards such pride as legitimate. In his view Christians have the right to be proud, not, admittedly, because of what they themselves are or accomplish, but certainly over the *cause* to which they have been won and which they now serve (Rom. 3:21–26; 5:1–11; and elsewhere). Their boasting is about the treasure they contain, not about the earthenware pot in which they contain it (2 Cor. 3:4—4:18). "Let him who boasts, boast of the Lord" (1 Cor. 1:31 RSV; 2 Cor. 10:17). On the other hand, Paul criticizes all boasting of one's own achievements and all righteousness based on one's own merits in terms which could scarcely be more devastating (Rom. 11:17–18; 1 Cor. 1:26–31; 4:7; and elsewhere).

These are ideals. But it is not simply a description of how things *should* be. Paul's starting point is his knowledge of what the situation in fact *is*; God's grace and calling are for him very real. Christians *are* children of light, and so forth. The admonitions amount to charges that they live up to what they, by the grace and provision of God, really are; that they—spiritually speaking—live according to their status. Paul perceived the actual state of affairs in his congregations clearly and without illusions. Often he has to address problems of moral weakness, carnality, and sins of various kinds. There was certainly good reason to repeat—as Paul does—again and again the admonitions to "put off" or "put away" those characteristics and deeds which marked the previous, heathen way of life ("the old man") and to "put on" those characteristics and deeds which mark life "in Christ" (see the discussion above). Thus, in judging Gentiles outside the church—those who are still the helpless prey of their "old man"—Christians have cause to examine themselves and to bear in mind their own frailty.

In texts of this kind, then, Paul depicts an ethos that is exclusively Christian; but this certainly does not mean that his is a simple, fixed ethos permitting neither variation nor pluralism.

A significant factor in this context is Paul's inability to argue from a *simple* moral gauge. He has broken with the idea that the law (Torah) is God's first and last word to the world. In the process he has also deprived himself of the possibility of using a simple, objectively accessible and eternally valid standard for determining in detail what is good and what evil, what is right and what wrong. Where the Spirit of God is, there is freedom. And where there is freedom, there is diversity.

It is thus significant and symptomatic when Paul speaks of the privilege and duty of Christians to test and decide within themselves what is "the will of God," what is "good and acceptable and perfect" (Rom. 12:2; Phil. 1:10; cf. Eph. 5:17; Col. 1:9); typical too is his respect for the individual's conscience (Romans 14; 1 Corinthians 8—9). In spite of the fact that one's conscience leads one to a conclusion different from someone else's in certain matters, one's conscience is one's own judge. The Lord alone is superior, the "supreme court." For Paul it is permissible, proper, and important that Christians discuss, instruct, inform, and admonish one another even in matters of conscience; he himself makes frequent use of opportunities to do so. But he firmly holds to the position that in the final analysis, individuals are bound by their own consciences. Paul is—for his own part—convinced that the consciences of "the weak" reach faulty verdicts, but he protects them from the encroachments of "the strong" (Romans 14; 1 Corinthians 8—9). On the other hand, he protects the consciences of "the strong" as well. "The weak" have no right to rule over the consciences of "the strong," limit their freedom, or contest their verdicts. The conviction of the individual conscience is here—in spite of the fact that it leads to differing opinions—recognized in a quite remarkable way. "Whatever does not proceed from faith [here "conviction of conscience"] is sin" (Rom. 14:22–23 RSV).

Does this mean Paul advocates an unchecked ethical subjectivism? The answer is no. Certain invariables of ethical judgment remain, certain truths about good and evil which are generally recognized and about which no discussion is needed. There are, for example, certain types of behavior which are and remain incompatible with the Spirit and with the nature of the reign of heaven. "The works of the flesh are *obvious* (*phanera*): immorality, impurity, licentiousness, idolatry, sorcery, enmity, strife, jealousy, anger, selfishness, dissension, party spirit, envy, drunkenness, carousing, and the like" (Gal. 5:19–21). Of such patent manifestations of worldly carnality Paul says "in advance"—that is, before the judgment—that they exclude the doer from God's kingdom. On the other hand, certain attitudes and ways of behaving can immediately be classified as genuine products of the Holy Spirit: "the fruit of the Spirit is love, joy, peace, patience, kindness, goodness, faithfulness, gentleness, self-control" (Gal. 5:22–23 RSV). Since, then, there is a basic foundation of consistent expressions both for what the sinful "flesh" desires and for what the "Spirit" desires, Paul can teach others in questions of morality and even use fairly fixed text material in so doing, such as the catalogs of virtues and vices (2 Cor. 6:6; Gal. 5:22–23; cf. 1 Tim. 4:12; also Rom. 1:29–31; 1 Cor. 6:9–10; 2 Cor. 12:20; and so forth).

Since the ethos which the Spirit produces "in Christ" can be traced in rough outline and described with the help of particular—indeed, already existing—words expressing moral judgments, there is a basis for a further question: did early Christianity share any ethical values with the Hellenistic milieu in which it was active? The many general statements which were referred to above and which speak of the darkness of the heathen could of course leave the impression that early Christianity's ethos was its own exclusive property.

Paul can write in the following terms to one of his congregations, "Whatever is true, whatever is honorable, whatever is just, whatever is pure, whatever is lovely, whatever is gracious, if there is any excellence, if there is anything worthy of praise, think about these things" (Phil. 4:8 RSV). The reasoning is based on the assumption that in God's world there are still among human beings values which are rightly held in honor, such things as nobility of spirit, generosity, purity, reliability—virtues and qualities which are pleasing and appreciated, to put what is said somewhat freely—and that Christians are to cultivate and promote things of this kind. This line of thought, and the many terms for moral values here taken from the Hellenistic world, show that there is a fundamental accord between the ethical ideals of Christians and those of their environment. Similarly, a common foundation of values is presupposed when Paul exhorts his fellow Christians to live irreproachably before those outside the church (Rom. 12:17; 2 Cor. 8:21; 1 Thess. 4:10–12; 5:15; 2 Thess. 3:7–13; and elsewhere). Naturally, this would be impossible if the values of outsiders were so perverted that they saw something evil in everything good, something wrong in all that is right. The apostle thus is convinced that neither the law of the Jews nor the ethical sensibilities of the heathens will be able to find behavior governed by the Spirit anything other than good. He is sure that the one who, in "righteousness and peace and joy in the Holy Spirit," serves Christ, not only pleases God but also is approved by men (Rom. 14:17–18 RSV).

Early Christianity's ethos did not contrast with that of the world around as white with black. Paul did not mean that God had totally withdrawn his hand from the heathens; the task of Christians not to be "conformed to this world" (Rom. 12:1–2) was thus not a requirement to be different at every point. In spite of his gloomy picture of the moral conditions of the heathen world, the apostle did think there were points of connection and correspondence between the good which early Christianity was intent on spreading and that which the heathens at least deep down in their hearts recognized as good (cf. the point of view expressed in Romans 1—2). He even thought that Christians could argue their cause before outsiders (Col. 4:5–6). The meaningfulness in all this becomes apparent when we compare early Christianity's ethos with that of the Hellenistic philosophers and teachers of wisdom. They have much in common.

A further point worth observing is that the ethos commended by Paul is free from ritual rules which lead to isolation. This too led to a simplifying of communication with outsiders and a facilitating of understanding.

In conclusion, perhaps an external judgment should be noted. Early Christianity did not go out into the world with an ethos to be realized at the cost of others. At the heart of this ethos was a love which neither makes demands of others nor lives at their expense but gives itself for others and to others. The ethical program of the Christians was meant in the deepest sense to bring others *gain*, not loss. Admittedly, such an ethos may provoke hatred on the part of outsiders—betrayed ideals lead to feelings of guilt within a person and resentment toward those who do not betray them—but the inner conviction that such an ethos is *beneficial* will not be silenced. An ethos with this aim ought to be able to command universal recognition, even from those who for their own part choose not to pursue it.

LOYALTY AND CONTRIBUTION
TO SOCIETY

Since his ideal is for liberated people not to "please themselves" but in love to sacrifice themselves for others, Paul finds it natural to admonish his "brothers in the faith" to shoulder of their own free will burdens and obligations, certain of which are fixed. They are, for example, to be subject to the political authorities and carry out that which the law and order of society demand. This submission too is to take place voluntarily—with inner freedom and personal responsibility intact. It is not a matter of blindly obeying orders. Political devilry is not forgotten. Here too the words "Do not become slaves of men!" (1 Cor. 7:23 RSV, emphasis added) apply;

here too the heavenly command must be supreme. The demands of earthly rulers can thus be carried out only to a specific limit; where loyalty to Christ is hazarded, the demands of human beings cannot be obeyed. But undeniably these demands, with their objective, obligatory character (notice the word "obligations," *opheilai*, in Rom. 13:7), come very near to placing a direct limitation on the Christian's freedom. In other words, on the external plane where these demands lie, freedom is in practice reduced.

Paul often stresses to his congregations that Christians are to fulfill their duties on this level. They are not to withdraw in an isolation imposed by vanity or, indeed, in sheer laziness from the task of carrying their part of the common burden; on the contrary, they are—of their own free will—to bear more than their share (cf. Gal. 6:2). They are to "do good to all men" (Gal. 6:10 RSV; and elsewhere). They, like all others, are to work for their livelihood (2 Thess. 3:6–13). "Owe no one anything," a typical maxim states (Rom. 13:8 RSV; cf. 1 Thess. 4:11–12). Here too we may note the command to be subject to the political "powers that be," a command which is formulated in such a general way as to include those occupying positions of authority of other types as well (Rom. 13:1–7; see further chapter one). Relevant here too are the exhortations in the *Haustafeln* that wives are to be subject to their husbands, slaves to their owners, children to their parents (Eph. 5:21—6:9; Col. 3:18—4:1; cf. in the pastoral Epistles 1 Tim. 2:8–15; Titus 2:1–10). Early Christianity seems in fact to have maintained a quite unified praxis in these matters. A perceptive scholar—E. G. Selwyn—has been able to derive from the Pauline Letters, 1 Peter, and James, catechetical patterns which appear to have been widespread in early Christianity. In this catechetical material one particular *topos* treated this very matter of "subordination" (*hypotassesthai*). Moreover, Paul himself says that in all his congregations he lays down as a rule that all are to remain in the stations of life in which they were called, seeking neither to escape nor to emancipate themselves (1 Cor. 7:17–24).

What we above all see here is that Paul—like early Christianity in general—retains the traditional view that the order of society too is ordained by God, and that it makes legitimate demands for loyalty. This outlook may seem passive, but it should be remembered that the small groups of early Christians—always in the minority—were scarcely in a position to make their voices heard where political decisions were reached and laws established. Furthermore, thoughts of rebelling and attempting to seize earthly power were foreign to them; Jesus' approach was not that of power seizure but of sacrifice. But we note secondly that subordination takes place voluntarily and, in part, with new motivations. Submission to the rulers of society is to be yielded "for the sake of conscience" and with inner responsibility intact (Rom. 13:1–7; cf. too "for the Lord's sake" in 1 Pet. 2:13!). Wives are to be subject to their husbands "as to the Lord" (Eph. 5:22–24; Col. 3:18). Children are to obey their parents "in the Lord" (Eph. 6:1; Col. 3:20). Slaves are to be obedient to their masters "as to Christ" (Eph. 6:5–8; Col. 3:22–25). At the same time, those occupying positions of *superiority* who receive the apostle's instruction are given corresponding admonitions to let their roles bear the imprint of Christ. Husbands are to love their wives "as Christ loved the church and gave himself up for her" (Eph. 5:25–33 RSV; cf. Col. 3:19). Fathers are to raise their children in a way worthy of the Lord (Eph. 6:4; cf. Col. 3:21). Masters are to treat their slaves as they themselves want to be treated by their heavenly Master (Eph. 6:9; Col. 4:1).

The picture which here emerges is an unusually clear one. While the universal renewal still awaits God's time, already a renewal and transformation is beginning in the world, "in Christ." But it is a transformation *from within*: from within the heart or "mind" (*nous*) of the individual Christian, the one who is not "conformed to this world" (Rom. 12:1–2). It marks the church, which makes up the "body of Christ," pervaded by Christ's Spirit. It is spread to the rest of the human community, out into society, by men and women who, from within, liberated and free, give themselves in voluntary service to others. They bear witness to it and stand for it even in the presence of political rulers (1 Tim. 6:12–16 and elsewhere). The church and society continue to act like a body with many parts serving different functions, but an inner re-creation has begun. Impelled by this new inspiration, impelled by these new motivations for service in the church and in society, a development is bound to occur, changes of different kinds are bound to take place: much of the old will gradually but inevitably be thrust to the side, much that is new will arise. History shows that the values and ideals which were thus practiced and proclaimed would come to have far-reaching consequences; orders of society would be transformed, many laws changed.

Still, not even within the church does Paul allow the "freedom we have in Christ" to sweep away all that is old and create all things anew. His "vision," to be sure, is clear enough: "As many of you as were baptized into Christ have put on Christ. Here there is neither Jew nor Greek, here there is neither slave nor free, here there is not 'male and female'; for you are all one in Christ Jesus" (Gal. 3:27–28; cf. 1 Cor. 12:13; Col. 3:11). But in spite of this vision he does not abolish relationships of subordination within the church: he stresses that wives are still to be subject to their husbands, children to their parents, slaves to their masters. The link with the order of society in early Christianity's environment is transparent; a parallel is Paul's respect for the principle that subjects are to be subordinate to those in authority. Perhaps most striking is the fact that early Christianity did not allow women the right of expression in congregational meetings: "Just as women in all the other churches of the saints keep silence, so they are to be silent in your meetings. For they are not permitted to speak, but should be subordinate, as even the law says." They are not even to ask questions in public: "If there is anything they desire to know, let them ask their husbands at home. For it is shameful for a woman to speak in church" (1 Cor. 14:34–36 RSV). (Praying and prophesying, however, were permitted. Neither the reciting of prayers nor prophesying required special permission for public utterance.) We see that Paul—like early Christianity in general—avoids letting emancipation run a free course, a course which would have created unrest in Jewish communities and in Roman society and which would have brought the church into disrepute. The main principle in such external questions of church order was that "all things should be done decently and in order" (1 Cor. 14:40 RSV). That the apostle's views would in the course of time bring changes was nonetheless inevitable. He had planted. Others would water. And the growth would come from all life's Source.

On the other hand, the attitude that for the sake of the great *cause* Christians represented they should avoid unnecessary conflicts with authorities and the order of society has proven to carry with it problems of its own. It has been liable to the misuse of showing uncritical accommodation or at least passivity in cases where bold, uncompromising confrontation might well have corresponded better with that for which the church ultimately stands.

It is in fact rather noteworthy that Paul, whose individual ethics were so radical, showed so little radicalism in his social ethics. But such indeed is the Paul of the Epistles. Presumably this was one of the reasons why the more developed Paulinism reflected in the pastorals seems to have gone a long way toward becoming "bourgeois."

THE PROBLEM OF HALAKHA FORMATION
IN THE CHURCH

Faithful to his view of Christian freedom, Paul did not believe he had the right to act as a dictator over the faith of other Christians (2 Cor. 1:24; cf. 1 Cor. 3:5). He could at times speak humbly, even disparagingly about himself (for example, 1 Cor. 15:9). Still, he viewed his office highly and maintained with no little pride the importance of his role in salvation history (Rom. 11:13; 15:15–21; 1 Cor. 15:10; and elsewhere). Naturally his words carried great weight from the very beginning among those who received them. It was natural too for his teaching to be spread orally and for his letters to be copied and read in churches other than those to which they were first directed. Similarly, it was natural that in time many of his letters were gathered and used for teaching in the church as a whole. But this process led to consequences which, with a view to the apostle's own basic principles, there is reason to examine.

In his letters, the apostle—like a father or an older brother—had to preach and teach, exhort and rebuke, answer questions and give advice. Some of the words he wrote and the directions he gave were so grounded in the principles at the heart of his message that their general applicability was present from the very beginning. But there were other things in the letters too: exhortations suited to a particular occasion; instructions which needed to be given, and which were given, with a particular recipient in mind. When the letters were shifted from their original anchoring in a definite situation, and especially when they were put on a level with the "sacred

Scriptures" of old and thus began to be read and interpreted, if not in a totally new way, certainly in a way somewhat *different* from what was the case at first—when this happened, it became more difficult to distinguish in the apostle's words between what was of greater and what of lesser significance, between what was fundamental and what occasional, between that which had a profound general applicability and that which was said with reference to quite specific circumstances.

A similar development can be traced in the matter of the apostle's efforts as organizer and counselor of the church. It was necessary to provide the newly founded Christian congregations with a certain organization. All community life—including the religious—must have organization and order. And order in the community is regarded in the Bible as something good: "For God is not a God of confusion but of peace" (1 Cor. 14:33 RSV). For the most part we can only guess how the congregations were structured. When Paul writes his letters, he shows very little interest in questions of church organization; his remark in 1 Cor. 11:34b is typical. Presumably the older congregations, especially the mother church in Jerusalem, have served as models, at least in a general way (cf. 1 Cor. 14:36; 1 Thess. 2:14). On certain points Paul did deliberately strive to create a unified praxis "in all the churches of the saints" (1 Cor. 4:17; 7:17; 11:16; 14:33–38). But a rigid and general uniformity seems to be foreign to him.

The newly converted needed teaching and models of behavior for their conduct as well. The picture we get of the apostle and his co-workers is that they are eagerly and busily involved in teaching and exhorting. This is apparent not only from the letters as a whole but also from specific texts where instruction about the Christian life style is directly mentioned (for example, Rom. 6:17; 1 Cor. 4: 16–17; 1 Thess. 4:1–8; 2 Thess. 3:6–12). Paul at times uses his authority to present himself as a pattern for imitation in all respects (1 Cor. 4:15–17; 11:1–2; 1 Thess. 1:6–8; 2 Thess. 3:6–12; and elsewhere). The admonition to imitate can be formulated very generally: "So then, brethren, stand firm and hold to the traditions which you were taught by us, either by word of mouth or by letter" (2 Thess. 2:15 RSV). At times the admonition becomes a sweeping recommendation to follow the attitudes and behavior cur-

rent among the dominant Christian leaders: "Brethren, join in imi-
tating me, and mark those who so live as you have an example in
us" (Phil. 3:17 RSV). Here Paul applies the pedagogy and methods
of transmission in which he himself has been trained. Naturally,
much has been changed. His primary concern is that his readers and
hearers will imitate his *faith* and his *love*; attention is here not so
strongly focused on individual details in his way of life. Still, the
exhortation to do as he does is formulated in such a general way
that he must have been imitated in such matters as well.

The apostle's written teaching, the direction he gave with regard
to church organization, his pedagogical references to the life style
which he and his fellow workers practiced—all these were natural
measures to take in the immediate situation. But at the same time,
processes were set in motion which—if allowed to proceed unchecked—might well blunt the very point at the heart of the
apostle's message and what was basic to his intentions. The written
way in which he formulated himself was fixed and not subject to
change when the letters were spread and read in completely new
situations. Church organization under Paul's direction had grown
up in particular historical circumstances, perhaps many times for
simple reasons inherent in the situation and without any deeper
motivations; now it became a pattern which was spread and copied
by churches in quite different circumstances. The original apostolic
life style was established as the *only* true Christian life style.

We recognize these processes from the general history of religions.
Religious institutions, ritualized religious acts, and standardized religious behavior are extraordinarily difficult to abolish or reform,
even when their original motivation no longer applies and when, in
principle, dogma permits freedom. In the case of early Christianity,
a *Christian halakha* began to take shape from the very beginning, a
new network of commands and standardized patterns of behavior
and action, which soon became established as the *only* life style
thought worthy of a Christian. Through the mechanisms of institutionalization and routinization, Christ and his apostles were made
into lawmakers and halakhists. No hesitation was shown in speaking
of Christ's new law (*nova lex*). Then too, the risk that inherited
patterns of behavior within the church would become rigidly fixed
increased as the Christian congregations were subjected to pestering

and persecution from without. Not all had the courage and strength of Jesus and Paul to expose themselves with supreme inner freedom and control to attacks, continuing their work with a vulnerable openness. Self-defense and increasing rigidity were natural human reactions.

Still, because the wording of the original writings has been preserved, we can see for ourselves what kind of an ethos was enjoined from the beginning. We find statements of principle, not least from the "apostle of liberty," which ought to prevent anyone from making of his words new yokes of slavery to cancel freedom "in Christ," quench the Spirit, and blunt the gospel. The apostle's reasons for defending "the freedom we have in Christ" were rooted in profound and fundamental convictions. His "vision" was a law-free—and therefore guilt-free—sphere, in which the Spirit can create "righteousness and peace and joy" and produce "a faith which is active in love." With regard to the "works of the flesh" which exclude people from God's kingdom, external laws and commands and statutes do little more in the apostle's view than conceal and—deep down—increase them. But where the Spirit is, there the "works of the flesh" are reduced to rudiments with little attractiveness to compare with "the fruit of the Spirit."

BIBLIOGRAPHICAL NOTE

For a broader, more detailed study of Pauline ethics, there is an abundance of literature. The following works may be mentioned: R. Bring, *Christus und das Gesetz* (Leiden: Brill, 1969); Lucien Cerfaux, *The Christian in the Theology of St. Paul* (New York: Herder & Herder, 1967); E. Eidem, *Det kristna livet enligt Paulus* (Uppsala: SKDB, 1927); V. P. Furnish, *Theology and Ethics in Paul* (Nashville: Abingdon Press, 1968); A. Grabner-Haider, *Paraklese und Eschatologie bei Paulus* (Münster: Aschendorff, 1968); R. Hasenstab, *Modelle paulinischer Ethik* (Mainz: Matthias-Grünewald Verlag, 1977); Bengt Holmberg, *Paul and Power: The Structure of Authority in the Primitive Church as Reflected in the Pauline Epistles* (Philadelphia: Fortress Press, 1980); Ernst Käsemann, *Perspectives on Paul* (Philadelphia: Fortress Press, 1971); R. Kieffer, *Le primat de l'amour: Commentaire épistémologique de 1 Corintiens 13* (Paris: Editions du Cerf, 1975); O. Merk, *Handeln aus Glauben: Die Motivierungen der paulinischen Ethik* (Marburg: N. G. Elwert, 1968); F. Mussner, *Theologie der Freiheit nach*

Paulus (Freiburg, Basel, Vienna: Herder, 1972); L. Nieder, *Die Motive der religiös-sittlichen Paränese in den paulinischen Briefen,* (Munich: K. Zink, 1956); W. Schrage, *Die konkreten Einzelgebote in der paulinischen Paränese: Ein Beitrag zur neutestamentlichen Ethik* (Gütersloh: Gütersloher Verlagshaus Gerd Mohn, 1961). For the link between 1 Corinthians 13 and Deut. 6:4–5, see my article "1 Kor. 13," in *Donum gentilicium* (D. Daube *Festschrift*) (Oxford: Clarendon Press, 1978), pp. 185–209. The reference in the text to O. Linton is to his articles "Den paulinska forskningens bada huvudproblem," in *Svensk Teologisk Kvartalskrift* 11 (1935): 115–41, and "Paulus och juridiken," in *STK* 21 (1945): 173–92. For the reference to H. Preisker, see his *Das Ethos des Urchristentums,* 2d. ed. (Gütersloh: C. Bertelsmann, 1949), pp. 165–94. The reference to E. G. Selwyn is to his book *The First Epistle of St. Peter* (London: Macmillan, 1946), pp. 363–466. See also the bibliography at the close of this book. I would like to mention particularly my indebtedness to the section on Paul in Rudolf Bultmann's *Theology of the New Testament* (New York: Charles Scribner's Sons, 1951; London: SCM Press, 1952), 1:185–352.

5

Early Christianity's Ethos
According to John

DISTANCE AND SIMPLIFICATION

The reader who comes to John from Paul or the synoptic Gospels senses that the perspective now is one of greater distance. The view has become clearer, the contours simpler and sharper. The evangelist chooses a limited number of episodes from Jesus' earthly ministry but, by way of compensation, lets Jesus interpret them. Even the subject matter of Jesus' words has been concentrated on a few crucial themes which are given extended treatment. The Johannine Jesus does not discuss concrete questions of the law—including ethical concerns—with his opponents. Everything centers on fundamentals: the Son is now in the world; he is rejected by many and received by a few. From his distant perspective, the evangelist is not concerned to distinguish particular historical groups surrounding Jesus (scribes, Pharisees, Sadducees, and so forth). The opponents constitute a single, dark out-group: "the Jews." It is apparent that the Johannine church understands itself as clearly distinct from "the Jews." Christians no longer have a part in the fellowship of the synagogue (cf. John 9:22, 12:42, 16:2). Even the Torah ("the law") is described in distancing formulas: it belongs to the Jews (John 7:19; 8:17; 10:34; and so on). It is not even mentioned in the Epistles or Revelation. Not that the Johannine church repudiates the ancient sacred writings; the Old Testament retains its significance when rightly interpreted as a witness to the Son. Moses and the prophets have testified of him (John 1:17, 45; 5:39). But the status and function of the law are no longer problematic. The period of the law is over, that of "grace and truth" has come (1:17). The real struggle with "the ethos of the Jewish theocracy" lies in the past.

The Johannine church is located in Asia Minor. This is evident in Revelation from the churches mentioned in chapters 1—3. And much in the Johannine writings shows how stimulating influences—images and ideas—from Hellenistic corners ("gnosis") have been taken up in the Johannine circle. Nonetheless the heritage from Palestine—and from Jesus—is unmistakably present and decisive. Who it was who passed it on is hard to say. It seems to have been a disciple very close to Jesus, "the beloved disciple" (19:26, 35; 21:20, 24). However, the Johannine writings—with the possible exception of Revelation—were not written by him, but by the circle surrounding him. Presumably the same man wrote the Gospel (chapters 1—20) and the First Epistle, another man wrote the other two Epistles, and a third Revelation. The Palestinian heritage does not show signs of direct links with Pharisaism, but rather with sectarian circles whose notions resemble those we now know from Qumran. It is, however, impossible to clearly demarcate the limits of Palestinian materials within the body of the texts.

In what follows, I deal with the writings as we have them and concentrate primarily on the Gospel and First Epistle. I call the author of these two writings "John" without discussing the question who he might have been.

The Johannine way of speaking about "the Jews" has been exploited for anti-semitic purposes. This is in fact a misuse. In all probability the authors of the Johannine writings were Jews themselves, and their bitter words against "the Jews" are directed not against the Jews as a race but against Judaism as a religious entity (the Judaism which rejects Jesus). Still, this way of speaking does not invite imitation; it should be avoided.

THE "DUALISTIC" BASIS

At the close of the Gospel, John makes the purpose of his book explicit: he has written as he did in order "that you may believe that Jesus is the Christ, the Son of God, and that believing you may have life in his name" (20:31 RSV). A similar declaration is found at the beginning of the First Epistle even though the letter is hortatory in character (cf. 2:1): "The life was made manifest, and we saw it, and testify to it, and proclaim to you the eternal life which was with the Father and was made manifest to us" (1:2

RSV). Everything John writes centers around the person and work of Jesus Christ. There is truth in the statement that Johannine theology is nothing but Christology, and his Christology is his soteriology. "Ethics" can be found here as well, but only as one dimension of Johannine theology—a fact I shall respect in what follows.

The Johannine writers have not been able to do without a salvation-historical framework. We see this, for example, in the prologue and in Jesus' farewell address in the Gospel, in a number of references in the letters, and—most strikingly—in the visions of Revelation concerning the future. Nevertheless it must be said that the total outlook is marked by a certain mythic timelessness. Here we meet a view of life characterized by sharp contrasts: light and darkness, life and death, truth and falsehood, freedom and bondage, righteousness and sin, above and below, and so on. The "world" (*kosmos*)—in John the word refers almost throughout to the "world of humankind"—has turned from God and is radically opposed to him. Admittedly, the whole world has been created by the one true God—through the Logos. It is worth noting the stress with which the prologue emphasizes that everything owes its existence to the Logos (John 1:1–3, 10). We are thus dealing not with an "ontological" but with a religious dualism. What has happened, according to the Johannine view, is that the world which God created has fallen away from God, losing in the process its true source of life, its link with light, life, truth, freedom. To be sure, it believes that it enjoys light, life, truth, freedom and that it knows what these things are, but in fact it is groping amid pure illusions. In its blindness it does not notice that it is shut up within itself and encompassed by darkness, a captive of mere false substitutes for the true light, true life, true freedom.

To this lost world God has sent his Son. The Son comes as a perfect representative of the Father in order to bring the world light, life, truth. As a concrete human being of flesh and blood he stands in a world which belongs to him, among people who are his. But he is rejected. "And this is the judgment, that the light has come into the world, and men loved darkness rather than light, because their deeds were evil" (John 3:19 RSV). "He was in the world, and the world was made through him, yet the world knew him not. He came to his own home, and his own people received him not" (John 1:10–11 RSV). In these tragic contrasts of black and white John depicts the fact that Jesus of Nazareth was rejected and executed.

Such is the broad perspective. Within it certain exceptions are pointed out. The world contains more than resistance and rejection. In it can be found also those who have received and do receive the Son of God. Of them is said, "But to all who received him, who believed in his name, he gave *exousia* (permission, authority) to become children of God" (John 1:12). The one who proceeds from the Father thus draws to himself those who are really the Father's children. Some give ear when the shepherd's voice sounds; they come to the light now that it appears before their eyes (John 3:20–21; 10:3–4, 27). And when they thus receive God's Son, they become the subjects of a radical transformation. Their life begins again, created anew. They experience a new "coming into existence." They are said to be "born again and from above" (the Greek word *anōthen* means both), "born of water and the Spirit" (John 3:3–8), "born of God" (John 1:13; 1 John 4:7; 5:4; and so forth); "God's seed" remains in them (1 John 3:9). Such is the extraordinarily radical way in which John views the transformation brought about by Jesus when he divides the masses of humanity into two.

Two things must here be emphasized.

1. When John speaks of the world in enmity with God, he is thinking primarily not of the "heathen" but of Israel. The traditional, all but ineffaceable boundary between Israel and the gentile nations has lost its crucial significance for John. The only line of demarcation which matters is that which divides those who are "of the truth," "of God," from those who are not. What takes place through the Son's ministry is that *true* Israelites are separated and gathered from the number of those called the people of God, and that their circle is complemented by Gentiles who prove to be "the children of God who are scattered abroad" (11:52 RSV). The true sheep who are found in the fold (that is, in Israel) are gathered together, and their number is completed by other sheep wandering outside the fold (10:16). The others remain in darkness and deceit. Without any real insight into what takes place in the darkness, those who are only apparently Israelites—John calls them "the Jews"—become one with Gentiles who are not "of God." Thus there is a

radical renewing of the people of God. A regrouping takes place; boundary lines are drawn differently from how they were before. It is a bitter portrayal which is painted of those who do not accept Jesus as Messiah.

2. John provides a few mysterious hints as to something lying beneath the surface, so to speak, of that which happens, hints which remind of Gnostic ways of referring to people who are, and remain, of different natures. Those who heed and follow at the sound of the Son's voice, thus showing themselves to be "of the truth," "of God," seem in some hidden way to be such already before their encounter with the Son. And of those who come to the Son it is said that they are those whom the Father "draws" to the Son (John 6:44) or "gives" to him (6:37; 17:6–9, 24). It is often said that Johannine "dualism" is a "decision dualism" (*Entscheidungsdualismus*): the division takes place first when people are forced to take a position with regard to the Son. It is difficult to judge the matter with any certainty, but it would seem that this interpretation is not the *whole* truth. It appears that John is falling back on certain notions of fate and predestination.

In the same way as the crowds are divided into two when the Son appears in Israel, so later people are divided through the activity of the church. John provides his readers with the following rule of thumb: "We are of God. Whoever knows God listens to us, and he who is not of God does not listen to us. By this we know the spirit of truth and the spirit of error" (1 John 4:6 RSV).

Through his unity with the Father (John 10:30 and elsewhere), the Son has and is the *true* light, life, freedom. The one who would find light, life, truth can find them in only one place in the world: in the Son. It is thus that the so-called "I am" sayings of Jesus in John's Gospel are to be interpreted: I—and nothing else—am the light of the world, the way, the truth, the life, the resurrection, the bread of life, the true vine, the good shepherd, the door to the sheep (6:35; 8:12; 10:7, 11; 11:25; 14:6; 15:1, and so forth).

That the Son is the *Logos* (John 1:1–5) means that he is not just God's "word" but also God's principle of life, the innermost secret behind everything and in everything which comes into existence and lives. Thus, those who come to the Son and "abide" in him have a share in all this, indeed, in God himself. This could be free, theoretical speculation. But for John it is the result of reflection about the actual conditions in which he and his churches find themselves.

At times the emphasis on the Son as the true revealer of God is so great and so exclusive that it almost sounds as though no secrets from the heavenly world had ever seeped out before Jesus appeared. "No one has ever seen God; the only Son, who is in the bosom of the Father, he has made him known" (1:18 RSV). "No one has ascended into heaven but he who descended from heaven, the Son of man" (3:13 RSV). "I am the door of the sheep. All who came before me are thieves and robbers" (10:7–8 RSV). But such sayings should not be pressed too far. Many texts indicate that John recognizes and relates positively to what was earlier revealed through Moses and the prophets (for example, 1:45; 5:39; 46). God has not spoken to his people *only* through his Son; it is the decisive, final word which has come through him, the word of grace and truth.

LOVE

According to the synoptic tradition, Jesus has adopted and radically pursued the principle that love (*agapē*) is the fundamental demand of God's law. In the Johannine writings, love has become the only ethical theme of significance. All ethical reflection centers around *agapē*.

The theme is treated—as we suggested earlier—theocentrically and Christocentrically. No other New Testament author says that "God is love," but John both says it and develops the idea in a consistent way. The statement is found in two places (1 John 4:8 and 16). It resembles a philosophical thesis about the essence of reality; in fact it is a characterization of God—and of a personal God—made by a reflective faith. More is meant than that "God loves." His very essence is love. Everything he does is dictated and motivated by love. It means as well—according to the Johannine way of thinking—that those who do not comprehend divine love do not yet know God (even though in many ways, both past and present, they have been the object of divine dealings). To learn to know God is to grasp his love. And to grasp his love is to receive a share in it, to be "infected" with it, so that one responds to it and allows oneself to be influenced by it. "He who does not love does not know God; for God is love" (1 John 4:8 RSV).

That which has revealed what God's innermost being is really like is the fact that his Son came into the world in the way he came, did the work he did, and met the fate he met. "In this the love of God was made manifest among us, that God sent his only Son into the world, so that we might live through him" (1 John 4:9 RSV). Thus it has become clear and plain that God's love is a radical giving of himself: "By this we know love, that he laid down his life for us" (1 John 3:16 RSV).

The sending of the Son into the world is depicted as an infinite sacrifice on God's part. In order to express what God had done when he allowed the innocent Christ to die, early Christianity utilized formulas from the traditions about Abraham's unlimited willingness to sacrifice to God (Genesis 22). In the ancient patriarchal society, a man's life lived on in the person of his sons. For a man to sacrifice his only son meant to sacrifice his own life. This ancient expression for a radical outpouring of oneself and an unlimited willingness to sacrifice was taken up by early Christianity and—with some liberty—applied to God's love. "For God so loved the world that he gave his only Son . . ." (John 3:16).

There is a speculative profundity in the Johannine statements about the Father's eternal love for the Son and the Son's for the Father. "You loved me before the foundation of the world," Jesus says in his high-priestly prayer (John 17:24), and similar statements are made elsewhere (for example, John 3:35; 5:20; 14:31; 15:9). But primarily what the Son's work in the world reveals is the relation between God and humankind.

First both in time and importance in this relation is the love of God for human beings, not that of human beings for God. "In this is love, not that we loved God but that he loved us and sent his Son to be the expiation for our sins" (1 John 4:10 RSV). The thought here is not that expiation and forgiveness took place simply at one isolated point in time when Jesus died; they are living realities even in the present. The present tense is clear; the Son lives now: "If anyone does sin, we have an advocate with the Father, Jesus Christ the righteous; and he is the expiation for our sins, and not for ours only but also for the sins of the whole world" (1 John 2:1–2 RSV).

The love which thus is God's fundamental trait must also characterize, inspire, and motivate his children. The one who belongs to

God and "abides" in him is to be like him. It is not a matter of superficial imitation of certain actions, but of conformity with the Son—even sharing his essential character. The same divine love which motivated Jesus Christ is to motivate his followers. If God is love, and God's Son is love, then God's children must also be love. If one is without the divine love, then one is without God, born merely of the world and the flesh. God is love's source. Where love is, it has been received from God and is an indication of fellowship with God. "Love is of God, and he who loves is born of God and knows God" (1 John 4:7 RSV; cf. 3:9–10; 4:15–16). This is stated as a description of a state of affairs. But the same point can be made as a demand, an ethical obligation: "If God so loved us, we also ought to love one another" (1 John 4:11 RSV). "He who says he abides in him ought to walk in the same way in which he walked" (1 John 2:6 RSV).

When one summarizes all that John says about love, it is not clear exactly what he means by "God's love" (*hē agapē tou theou*). He appears not to make any clear distinction between God's love for "us" and "our" love for God. We are really dealing with the mysterious "God-love"—a love which comes from God and is expressed in the Father's love for the Son and the Son's love for the Father, in the Father's and the Son's love for the "world," and in the response this love rouses in those who receive the Father through the Son. The problem can be studied in such texts as John 5:42; 15:9–10; 1 John 2:5; 3:17; 4:12.

In Old Testament times no distinction was drawn between the *fear* of God and *love* for God. In Jesus' time, however, scribes had begun to discuss whether love (*ahavah, agapē*) was not something greater and more important than fear (*jirah, phobos*). Probably we hear an echo of these discussions in John's words "There is no fear in love, but perfect love casts out fear. . . . He who fears is not perfected in love" (1 John 4:18 RSV).

THE NEW COMMANDMENT

Thus the love of Christ is the pattern and motivation for that of Christians. They are said to have received "a new commandment" from Jesus to love each other. It is not completely clear in what respect the commandment is *new*. Essentially two things seem to be involved.

1. *Direction.* The old command of love toward one's neighbor (Lev. 19:18) required loyalty within the boundaries of one's own nation (Israel); the new commandment of love for the "brethren" ("one another") requires loyalty within the new fellowship of those who follow Jesus—all Christians, regardless of their national origins. In ancient times it was difficult to detach oneself from one's natural relationships and allow some other fellowship to take their place. The command to love the "brethren" of the same faith is thus no easy matter.

2. *Character.* The new command is given with a concrete model: Jesus, who gave himself in a radical way to death for the sake of those he loved. In John 13:34–35, the Johannine Jesus says: "A new commandment I give to you, that you love one another; even as I have loved you, that you also love one another. By this all men will know that you are my disciples, if you have love for one another" (RSV). The same theme is developed in 15:12–17; 1 John 2:7–11; 3:11–17; 4:19–21. The radicalness of Jesus' exemplary love is indicated in a crucial saying which in itself may be adapted from an older phrase with probable earlier links with the *Shema*: "Greater love has no man than this, that a man lay down his life for his friends" (John 15:13 RSV). It is hardly justified to raise the criticism just at *this* point that love for enemies is still greater (cf. Rom. 5:6–8). Such a comparison is not here in view. The point being made is that it is impossible to give a greater proof of love than to sacrifice one's most precious possession—life itself—for another. The love enjoined by Jesus' "new commandment" is thus to be of the same kind and to have the same direction as that of Jesus himself: "we ought to lay down our lives for the brethren" (1 John 3:16 RSV).

Nonetheless it is striking that the extent of the love commandment indicated in the Johannine formulations is so *narrow*: love for "the brethren" (*hoi adelphoi*), love for "one another," sacrificing one's life for "the brethren." There are statements in the Johannine writings that give the impression of a complete universalism: God is love, God has created the whole world (through the Logos, John 1:3, 10), he loves the "world" and has sent his Son to save the "world" (John 3:16–17; 12:47; 1 John 2:2; 4:14). It would be possible on the basis of these great statements about God's essence and his creative and redemptive activities to argue for an attitude completely characterized by love: love for all, love for the whole world. And there *are* statements in the Johannine writings which in themselves can be taken as speaking of a love which is universal, crossing every boundary. "He who does not love does not know God; for God is love" (1 John 4:8 RSV). But such statements are few, and it is doubtful whether they really are meant in any universalistic way. The easy shift from the broad expression "the world" to the limited "the one who believes" in John 3:16 is worth noting: "For God so loved the world . . . that *whoever believes in him* should . . . have eternal life" (RSV, emphasis added). A similar shift from "the world" to "us" can be noted in 1 John 4:9: "In this the love of God was made manifest among us, that God sent his only Son into the world, so that *we* might live through him" (RSV, emphasis added). By "we" is meant not humankind but those who receive the Son.

The ethical duty of love for "the brethren"—the word "neighbor" (*ho plēsion*) is not found in the Johannine writings—is based on the actual situation which has arisen through the coming of the Son into the world. It has become apparent that the world does not want to know of God's offer. When light comes into the world, people's preference for darkness over light and their desire to remain in the darkness become evident. In its self-sufficiency, obduracy, and blindness, the world rejects the Son, repudiates and kills him. The fight is later carried on against his followers: hatred for God's Son is expressed in hatred for them (John 15:18–25 and elsewhere). It is in this situation of irreconcilable conflict between light and darkness, life and death, truth and falsehood, "us" and the world, that the command of "love for the brethren" is given.

The attitude toward the world is a negative one. Not that one dreams of being able to leave it, but one does separate oneself from it; note the key expressions "in the world" but not "of the world" in Jesus' farewell address (John 17:11–19). The dissociation is a radical one: "We know that we are of God, and the whole world is in the power of the evil one" (1 John 5:19 RSV). The prince of this world is none other than Satan (John 12:31; 14:30; 16:11), and those who are of the world are children of the devil (John 8:44; 1 John 3:8, 10). The disciples do, however, find comfort and courage in the knowledge that Jesus has "overcome the world" and destroyed the devil's works (John 16:33; cf. 1 John 3:8). "He who is in you is greater than he who is in the world" (1 John 4:4 RSV). It is impossible to miss the sense of superiority over the world in the Johannine writings. Jesus has "overcome the world" and given his followers part in his victory. "Whatever is born of God overcomes the world; and this is the victory that overcomes the world, our faith" (1 John 5:4 RSV). In the letters to the seven churches in Revelation, the situation of Christians in the world is portrayed as being one of extreme trial in which, however, they are intended to overcome. "He who conquers"—that is, in Jesus' strength remains faithful and thus stands the test in a situation of martyrdom— is promised a heavenly reward (Rev. 2:7, 11, 17, 26–28; 3:5, 12, 21).

The world, for all its inferiority, remains perilous territory nonetheless. For this reason it cannot be embraced by any spontaneous appreciation or bold and generous concern. In a double sense it is enemy soil. (1) It tempts and entices, it desires to keep men in its power, in darkness and deceit. Hence the exhortation "Do not love the world or the things in the world. If any one loves the world, love for the Father is not in him" (1 John 2:15–17 RSV). (2) It responds with fiery sanctions against those who withdraw from it or, more accurately, who are "taken" out of the world and "given" to the Son. With a deadly hatred the world persecutes those who depart from its ways (John 15:18–25; 17:14–16; cf. 1 John 3:11–12).

We note in John a sharp demarcation drawn between those inside and those outside the fold, a community awareness of a kind which reminds of the people of Qumran. But at Qumran the rule applies that one is to "love all the children of light and *hate* all the children of darkness." No corresponding exhortation is found in the Johannine writings. Here calm reflection prevails instead: "Do not wonder, brethren, that the world hates you" (1 John 3:13 RSV). "If the world hates you, know that it has hated me before it hated you," the Johannine Jesus says in his farewell address (John 15:18–19 RSV). Hatred against Christians is interpreted as hatred against Christ, hatred against God, and Christians are not told to hate in return. The exhortation which is given is a positive one. It requires unity and loyalty. What is needed is a love which unites those whom the world hates. Hence one is to love "the brethren," to love "one another" (1 John 3:11, 23; 4:7, 11, 12, and so forth). But John is evidently not prepared to go so far as to command love for one's enemies. Jesus' ideal of *boundless* love is naturally a difficult assignment to master in times of persecution.

For the background of the exhortations is quite clear. John is speaking to a church which meets with little toleration. It is hard pressed from without by hatred, badgering, and persecution. Even if the persecution reflected in the Gospel and Epistles seems not as serious as that we sense behind the Book of Revelation (1:9—3:22 and elsewhere), it is still serious enough. It is in such a situation that John insists on his urgent slogan "Love one another!" "Love the brethren!" It is a cry summoning each individual Christian to sincerity and endurance, and demanding unity and loyalty on the part of all while the darkness outside deepens and hatred sharpens its swords. What we see in the Gospel and the Epistles is not a "zeal" (*zēlos*) of the type which blazes in Revelation—an eschatologically motivated fervor not easy to distinguish from disguised vindictiveness. But neither is it the generous, boundless, indomitable love which we encounter in Jesus' words: "Love your enemies and pray for those who persecute you, so that you may be sons of your [boundlessly generous] Father who is in heaven" (Matt. 5:44-45 RSV).

The Christianity we meet in the so-called pastoral Epistles is very open toward the world and seemingly on the way to becoming bourgeois. This is hardly a risk run by the Christianity which the authors of the Johannine writings attempt to foster. The risk here is another: that of abandoning the world and withdrawing into the narrow confines of the "faithful." Later in the history of the church, narrow pietistic movements have been able to derive many a slogan from the urgent warnings of the Johannine writings as to the perils of the "world."

THE SHEMA?

John is in complete agreement with the synoptics in making the love (*agapē*) commandment the central one, linking in the process love for God with love for one's fellow human beings: "And this commandment we have from him, that he who loves God should love his brother also" (1 John 4:21 RSV). The question to which we now must turn is this: Does John deliberately and explicitly link the demand to love with the Old Testament command to love God, and with the *Shema,* the text in which this command is found?

Apparently he does not. Nowhere in the Johannine writings is Deut. 6:4–5 quoted. (The same is true of Lev. 19:18, which deals with love toward one's neighbor.) Possibly the statement that the love commandment is not only a "new" command but also an "old" one (1 John 2:7–8; 3:11–12; cf. 2 John 5) is meant to suggest such a linkage; more likely, however, what is meant is that it is an "old" command in the sense that the church has known the commandment from its beginning. In that case, the reference is simply to the "new commandment" of Jesus.

Naturally, however, we do find in the *traditional material* at John's disposal many fragments which indicate that his thoughts regarding love have their roots in the teaching of Jesus and his first disciples connected with the *Shema.* We are here dealing with scattered remnants from the characteristic mosaic pattern of this fundamental command. This is not the place for a thorough inventory of the material, but a few suggestions can be made. What we are looking for are motifs dealing with *unity* (the Lord is one), with *wholeness* (with your whole heart, and so forth), and with *obedience* ("hearing") and *love* marked by the *heart, soul,* and *strength* (the latter in the sense of external possessions).

It is clear in the Gospel that John deliberately repudiates the objection that Jesus represents a threat to faith in God as *one.* There is a strong emphasis—as we have already seen—on the view that Jesus does not exist alongside of or in conflict with God in any way, but that he is the Son, one with God and representing God in every respect. He has proceeded from the Father, and he says and does only what the Father sent him to say and do (for example, 3:34–35; 5:19–20). A good number of texts in John treat the matter. The most concise statement of the theme is found in the words "I and the Father are one" (John 10:30; cf. 10:38; 14:10–11; 17:21–22). The unity motif is even extended to include God's people, the church. The coming of the Son does not mean that God now has two peoples or a new people. The Son has simply called forth the *true* Israel, the true worshipers of the one true God, drawn from the nominal Israel and the Gentiles. Furthermore, the conviction that the true people of God shall be one with the Son, and hence one with the Father also, is strongly put (for example, John 17:11, 21–23).

Much could be said about the *wholeness* motif. In this context it will perhaps be sufficient to point to the radicalism seen throughout: all or nothing, black or white. The contrasts are sharp, and the Greek word *pas* ("every," "all") makes frequent appearances. On the other hand, the word *holos* ("whole"), which usually appears in the Greek versions of the *Shema* (the wording about one's "whole" heart, and so forth), does not occur in any phrase which could be traced to that text.

The *obedience* theme is so extensive and general that I shall not enter into a discussion of it here. The verb "to hear," "listen," "heed" (*akouein*) occurs some one hundred twenty times in the Johannine writings; on occasions the usage shows a close parallel with the *Shema*, though no specific linking with this text is apparent.

That *love* (*agapē*, corresponding to Hebrew *ahavah*) is the fundamental demand in John has already been discussed.

John is building on central parts of the Jesus tradition when he represents self-sacrifice in death as the greatest proof of love. Here, as we know, is a point at which early Christianity took up the phrase "You shall love the Lord your God . . . with your whole soul (*psychē*)," interpreted to mean "even if it costs you your life." It is undoubtedly from this context that the traditional formulation is taken: "Greater love has no man than this, that a man lay down his life for his friends" (John 15:13 RSV). The Johannine Jesus, in making this statement, is thinking of his own sacrifice; he develops the theme elsewhere (John 10:11–18) and even makes clear use of logia from the synoptic tradition in so doing (12:23–28). Hence one of the obligations which comes with discipleship of Christ is that of offering one's life, should the demand be made (ibid.). Jesus' attitude is presented in exhortations as an ideal requiring imitation: "By this we know love, that he laid down his life for us; and we ought to lay down our lives for the brethren" (1 John 3:16 RSV).

The demand that love is to govern one's use of external possessions (*mamon*; the word does not occur in the Johannine writings) also finds expression: "If any one has the world's goods [*bios*, "means of subsistence," "property"] and sees his brother in need, yet closes his heart against him, how does God's love abide in him?" (1 John 3:17 RSV).

The two quotations just cited are taken from a context rich in its associations with the *Shema*: 1 John 3:16–22. Still, it is hardly likely even here that John is consciously alluding to the *Shema*. We seem to be dealing with patterns of thought present in the traditional material of which John makes use in his exhortation. I have already mentioned the allusions to "soul" and "strength" (that is, possessions). In the same passage the heart (*kardia*) is also mentioned—a word John otherwise does not use except in a couple traditional phrases. In this text what is said about the heart is that we can have confidence before God "if our hearts do not condemn us," and that God may approve us even when "our hearts condemn us" (3:19–21). *Possibly* there may be certain associations here with the theme that our heart is not to be divided before God, but it is not self-evident.

In this same context we encounter as well the theme that one is not simply to "say" but also to "do": "Little children, let us not love in word or speech but in deed and in truth" (1 John 3:18 RSV). The theme that the commandment must be "done" is strongly emphasized in Deuteronomy, not least in the context of the command to love God in 6:5; it has thus a traditional association with the *Shema* as well. It is therefore of some interest that it too is found in this passage in 1 John.

"Desire," "lust" (*epithymia*), was often mentioned in connection with teaching on the "heart." John uses the word in a negative sense in only one context: in the borrowed phrases "lust of the flesh," "lust of the eyes," and "the world's lust" in 1 John 2:16–17. Only here in the Johannine writings is the word "flesh" (*sarx*) used in the negative sense which it usually bears in Paul. Elsewhere it is neutral. The "flesh" is earthly and mortal and therefore "of no avail" when it comes to "giving life" (John 3:6; 6:63; 8:15), but it is no more sinful than other earthly things.

107

Our study in this section has also confirmed that John does not write during Christianity's very earliest stages. The distance is apparent.

THE INDIVIDUAL CHRISTIAN

John shows no interest in concrete individuals or in concrete groups within the church; nor is his exhortation directed toward concrete problems in their religious life, still less in their civil and social life. When by way of exception he addresses "fathers," "young men," and "children" (1 John 2:13-14), the division is only rhetorical; the admonitions are of a general nature. John does of course distinguish a group when he speaks of false teachers, but this is only because the situation demanded it. He addresses not concrete individuals but the Christian individual as conceived "in principle."

It is illuminating in this regard to compare the Epistle of 1 John with that of James. In the latter Epistle the writer is a prophet and teacher who really intends to address different groups, shed light on different situations, and provide specific guidance for his readers in concrete areas of life. His language is concrete and forthright. In the 108 verses in the Epistle, 54 imperatives have been counted. John too is concerned to exhort, and he uses a number of imperatives in so doing. But the tone of what he has to say has rather the character of a meditative, intimate discussion—often in "we" form —and he speaks "in principle." He addresses the individual—so much is crystal clear—and appeals to the individual's own insights, but he is speaking not to different, concrete individuals but to every one in the congregation at the same time. We might speak of a *general*, as opposed to a *differentiated*, individualization.

Are we here simply dealing with meditation carried on at a distance from practical issues, with exhortations from one who has withdrawn from the concrete fellowship and from the concrete problems raised by active involvement? The suspicion is scarcely without warrant. But it must be balanced with a further observation. There is also a theological reason for John's attitude when he declines to tell his "dear children" what to do in the specific questions of life.

There was an old—and quite understandable—ideal that mature individuals ought to perceive for themselves what they are to do.

The will of God ought to be written in one's heart, so that there will be no need for being continually taught by others. We find this ideal in the famous chapter dealing with the new covenant in the Book of the Prophet Jeremiah: "And no longer shall each man teach his neighbor and each his brother, saying, 'Know the Lord,' for they shall all know me, from the least of them to the greatest, says the Lord" (Jer. 31:34 RSV). This theme about mature spiritual insight and independent ethical judgment on the part of every individual member of the people of God is expressed in a direct quotation from a similar prophetic text (Isa. 54:13) in John 6:45, and the ideal is suggested in a number of ways in different contexts. It was thus well-known in the Johannine circle. "But you have been anointed by the Holy One (that is, have received the Holy Spirit), and *you all have knowledge.*" "But the anointing which you received from him abides in you, and you have no need that any one should teach you; as his anointing teaches you about everything, and is true, and is no lie, just as it has taught you, abide in him" (1 John 2:20, 27 RSV).

It is thus clear from a number of texts that John respects the believing individual's own insight and responsibility, refraining from the meddlesome zeal which attempts to point out what should be done in all of life's concrete questions. He does not relieve his fellow Christians of their own responsibility. That he nonetheless exhorts them "in principle" is, of course, in a sense inconsistent, but it is an inconsistency which he shares with the whole of the New Testament. Even the apostle who respects the slogan "All of us possess knowledge" feels free to give warnings and advice like a father or older brother in the fellowship of Christians. We recognize the same state of affairs as we saw in Paul. John does the same, with a certain patriarchal benevolence: "my children."

THE CHURCH, FELLOWSHIP, TRADITION

We have seen how strongly individualized the exhortation of 1 John is—as strongly as is Jesus' demand in John's Gospel that individuals take a stand for him. But we have also seen that those who are addressed are not isolated individuals but members of the church, "brethren," "my children." The Johannine writings show little concern to *describe* the church, but they do contain classical pictures of it: the vine with its branches (John 15:1–6), the flock (John 10:11–18), and so on. Church awareness is strong in these writings. This is in part due to the "dualistic" outlook, and also to the conviction that unity is to be found in the Son: unity between God and those who have received the one he has sent; a fellowship of love embracing the Father, the Son, and the church.

None of the Johannine writings is of a missionary nature, directed toward outsiders. All are addressed to Christian congregations within the Johannine area, to the church. Not that John is oblivious to the church's missionary task. The Risen Lord appears to the church, not to the world (John 14:22), but he entrusts it with authority and a commission: "As the Father has sent me, even so I send you"; and he equips it with God's Holy Spirit (John 20:21–23; cf. 17:18). It is uncertain, however, whether the missionary zeal of the Johannine congregations was particularly strong at the time the writings were composed; quite likely persecution had dampened their boldness. The authors of these writings, however, have themselves maintained their confidence.

The *didactic* boldness and creativity of the Johannine church is reflected in Jesus' farewell address. The Johannine Jesus insists that his earthly ministry is to have a sequel which is to be led by the Holy Spirit (the "Spirit of Truth," "Paraclete"), who is to be given to the church (John 14—17). The peculiar qualities of John's Gospel are seen in their proper light when it is read with these chapters in mind. John shows confidence in the church's possession of the Spirit in his Epistle as well (1 John 3:24; 4:13). A further theme expressing this is that of the church's (the Christians') "abiding" (*menein*) in Christ (and God), as Christ (and God) abides in the church (Christians)—a theme to which we shall return shortly.

An important text for an understanding of the church in John is 1 John 5:6–9 (with allusions to John 1:32–34 and 19:33–37): "There are three witnesses, the Spirit, the water, and the blood; and these three agree" (v. 8 RSV). Here evidently the Spirit, Baptism, and the Eucharist are taken to be specially significant marks of the church.

For John, the place for the individual Christian's growth is within the fellowship of the congregation. The many exhortations to an active love for the brethren indicate that he is not at all thinking of a passive membership "in principle" only, but of actual participation in a fellowship that is living and warm. In speaking of the flock to which the Christian belongs (John 10) and the vine in which he must abide (John 15), John is referring primarily to fellowship with Christ; but fellowship with "the brethren" is obviously included.

The ethos we encounter in the Johannine writings is a *church ethos*. It demands, to be sure, a profound inward transformation of individuals, but it is assumed that this can take place only within the framework of the church's sacramental fellowship with Christ. To be saved from death and enter life, it is necessary to be baptized in water and "born" anew of the Spirit into a sphere where love prevails and where the Spirit causes a spring of living water to flow within each individual (John 7:37–39).

In a number of texts, John's hearers (the Gospel and Epistle were intended to be read aloud in the congregation) are exhorted to abide (*menein*) in God, in Christ, in the light, in love, and so forth (1 John 2:6, 10, 27, 28; 3:6, 24; 4:13, 16; and so forth). This is thus a *duty*. As a parallel to this we find the duty of "doing" God's will, "that which is well pleasing to him," the truth, righteousness, his commands; of "keeping" his commands or his words; or of "walking" according to his commands or in his commands, and so forth. These formulations are vague and lack contours; they are not given concrete application.

It is clear, however, that John is able to speak in such general, sweeping terms because *the congregations have already received the fundamental norms*; with these they are already familiar. This is apparent from a number of sayings: "For this is the love of God, that we keep his commandments" (1 John 5:3 RSV; cf. 2 John 6). "He who has my commandments and keeps them, he it is who loves me" (John 14:21 RSV; cf. 14:15, 24; 15:10). In Jesus' farewell address and high-priestly prayer (John 14—17) it is assumed that the disciples have received and therefore possess Jesus' words, Jesus' commands—which in fact are not his, but the Father's (John 12:49–50; 14:24; and so on); and in the Epistles we meet exhortations to abide in Christ's teaching (2 John 8–10), to which the congregation obviously has access already. The same thing is evident in the charge to "let what you heard from the beginning abide in you" (1 John 2:24 RSV), or to recall the new and yet already old commandment which the congregation has had since its beginning (1 John 2:7).

None of the Johannine writings is intended to provide elementary orientation for beginners. The churches have not been founded recently, nor has John been the only one to preach, instruct, and exhort in them. Unfortunately, we know very little as to how these churches were organized. Presumably, prophets and teachers did give concrete instructions for Christian living. In addition to this, ethical teaching would have been conveyed in more general ways; for example, by the reading of texts and other liturgy, by conversation and mutual admonition between brothers and sisters, by the very spirit prevailing within the churches. Here the church's tradition and the social pressure within the congregation, which took its character from the tradition—the pressure of the fellowship as a whole on the individual—must have had great significance, particularly inasmuch as the church dissociated itself from the rest of the world.

It is indeed striking how radically the ethos we meet in the Johannine writings repudiates the "world," that is, the values and patterns of living esteemed and pursued by people in general or—to use current cant—the value systems and structures into which the ordinary person is indoctrinated and by which he is manipulated. What one is exhorted to is not, however, violent struggle, rebellion, and seizure of power. Instead one is to wait for Christ's return, practicing in the meantime his radical pattern of living—that of sacrificial love. Since the light has been kindled in the world of darkness, it must continue to shine there.

The Johannine exhortation hardly makes the impression of being bourgeois, though certainly it is that of a conservative church. One is to "remain" what one has become (abide in Christ) and to retain that with which one has been entrusted (God's words and commands, Christ's words and commands). The exhortation is typical: "Let what you heard from the beginning abide in you. If what you heard from the beginning abides in you, then you will abide in the Son and in the Father" (1 John 2:24 RSV).

This, however, is not the same thing as rigidly preserving church tradition. The exhortations tend—as we have noted several times—

to emerge as a single inspiring admonition to love; that is, to a definite *spirit* which is to govern everything from within, taking expression in actions which bear the marks of love. The references to the words and commands of God and Christ do not constitute a charge to slavishly conform to the letter of carefully defined holy writings. What is suggested is that Christians must become better rooted, grow, and mature in that love which knows no equal. In Jesus' farewell address in the Gospel of John, it is said that the Spirit ("Paraclete") will carry Christ's work to completion (14:25–26; 15:26–27; 16:13–14). His task will thus be not simply to remind of what Jesus has said but also to clarify the divine revelation still further: "When the Spirit of truth comes, he will guide you into all the truth; for he will not speak on his own authority, but whatever he hears [from the Father] he will speak . . ." (John 16:13 RSV). John's Gospel itself evidences how creative the work of the Spirit was thought to be. In it Jesus' words and the narratives concerning him have been illuminated and amplified in a way striking in its freedom and creativity. The tradition has been retained, but it has been allowed to *live*.

A church ethos like the Johannine one may become a nervous pietism; alternatively, it may lead to a radical and bold renewal from within. Everything depends on which side of the matter is accentuated.

SIN WITHIN THE CHURCH

John (like Paul) has some difficulty explaining how *sin* can be present in the church. It is easy to see why. To be sure, what he says about the people of God, the true Israel, the church, is not meant to describe something which exists only as an ideal. John means to describe a reality: the people of flesh and blood who are God's people in this world. But since they represent what is "true" and "proper," they are inevitably portrayed in an idealized way with grandiose terms.

The picture John paints—as we have already noted—is one of black and white: the contrast is sharp between God and the devil, light and darkness, truth and falsehood. But John has difficulty combining this dualistic view of redemption—by which Christians are seen as born again of God, equipped with God's Spirit, abiding

113

in God, filled with divine love—with the thought that sin can be found within the church. His view of redemption compels him to say, "We know that any one born of God does not sin, but He who was born of God keeps him, and the evil one does not touch him" (1 John 5:18 RSV). "No one who abides in him sins; no one who sins has either seen him or known him." "He who commits sin is of the devil" (1 John 3:6, 8, RSV).

Such statements relate to the *essence* of the new life from God; they are statements of principles. On the other hand, the author of the Epistle has to say: "If we say we have no sin, we deceive ourselves, and the truth is not in us." "If we say we have not sinned, we make him a liar, and his word is not in us" (1 John 1:8, 10 RSV).

Here the argument seems to be based on the actual state of affairs, on an awareness of the frailty found in all things human, even in the sanctified. The fact of sin within the church and in the lives of Christians cannot be explained away.

In the same letter we find these two types of sayings side by side. To a certain extent the opposition between them is softened by words which strongly emphasize that the church and the Christian have continuous access to reconciliation and forgiveness: "If we confess our sins, he is faithful and just, and will forgive our sins and cleanse us from all unrighteousness" (1 John 1:9 RSV). Thus, according to John, sin has no abiding place within the church.

Hence John *admonishes* his "dear children"; he writes "that you may not sin" (1 John 2:1). The word "repentance" (*metanoia*) does not occur in the Johannine writings. That Christian congregations may be asleep and need to wake up and "repent" (verb: *metanoein*) is admittedly declared forcefully in Revelation (2:5, 16, 22; 3:3, 19), but similar admonitions are not found in either the Gospel or the Epistles.

In his letter of exhortation, John also shows his awareness of the self-judgment and self-condemnation of the scrupulous conscience and of the agony which feelings of guilt may cause. This leads him to focus attention on a higher court of justice: "If our hearts condemn us, God is greater than our hearts, and he knows everything" (1 John 3:20). This is certainly not to be interpreted as a reminder that the omniscient God is even sharper than the human heart in perceiving and condemning sin; the words are meant to bring comfort in the knowledge that the God who knows all things—including the frailty of human beings—is merciful, forgiving, willing to acquit. The preceding verse (3:19) makes this clear.

Forgiveness can be appropriated in the sacramental fellowship of the church with Christ, if sins are confessed (1 John 1:9; 2:1–2). John also emphasizes the responsibility of Christians for each other and their opportunities for helping each other. One such possibility is intercession: "If any one sees his brother committing what is not a mortal sin, he will ask, and God will give him life for those whose sin is not mortal" (1 John 5:16 RSV).

Here, however, John draws a limit. "There is sin which is mortal; I do not say that one is to pray for that" (1 John 5:16 RSV). There has been a good deal of discussion throughout the church's history as to what John can mean by the mortal sin for which there is no point in interceding. Presumably what is meant is such sin as leaves no doubt that the sinner is not and cannot be "of God," "born of God." We need not attempt to solve the problem here. What from an ethical point of view is worth noting is the fact that John places a boundary on concern for one's brother which is to apply even in the matter of intercession. We have pointed out earlier that Jesus' radical ideal of love is cut short by John in that he does not enjoin love for sinners, enemies, and persecutors. A second example of this reduction is seen in these words that one need not pray for those guilty of mortal sin. A third example from Johannine circles is found in Revelation, with its stringent requirements of rigorous church discipline against false teachers (Rev. 2:6, 14–16, 20–22). The eschatologically motivated "zeal" (*zēlos*) which here finds expression is not quite compatible with Jesus' demands for love and prayer which know no bounds. In Revelation we even find examples of a disguised vindictiveness against the world (19:11–21) and a fateful "keep it up": "The time is near. Let the evildoer still do evil, and the filthy still be filthy" (Rev. 22:10–11 RSV). The Epistles too contain instructions about the use of church discipline against false teachers, though in a milder form (2 John 10–11).

In his classical work dealing with the Christian conception of love through the ages (*Agape and Eros*), A. Nygren notes that John has provided us with our finest formulations of what *agapē* is; he has given the motif its final form; but at the same time he has also softened and reduced the motif in certain respects. It is undeniably with such a double impression that one is left after studying the ethical dimension of these writings from the unknown man traditionally called "the apostle of love."

BIBLIOGRAPHICAL NOTE

The Johannine "visions" and problems associated with individual texts can be studied in the fairly recent commentaries to John's Gospel by R. E. Brown and R. Schnackenburg. The latter has also written a fine commentary on the Johannine Epistles, the former is preparing one. With regard to Johannine ethics, I would refer in part to the general works mentioned in the list of literature which concludes this book, particularly those concerned with the *agapē* motif; also to the following special studies: M. L. Appold, *The Oneness Motif in the Fourth Gospel* (Tübingen: Mohr, 1976); J. Heise, *Bleiben: Menein in den johanneischen Schriften* (Tübingen: Mohr, 1967); N. Lazure, *Les valeurs morales de la théologie johannique* (Paris: Lecoffre, J. Gabalda et Cie, 1965); M. Lattke, *Einheit im Wort: Die spezifische Bedeutung von "agapæ," "agapan," und "philein" im Johannesevangelium* (Munich: Kösel-Verlag, 1975); S. Pancaro, *The Law in the Fourth Gospel* (Leiden: Brill, 1975); O. Prunet, *La morale chrétienne d'après les écrits johanniques* (Paris: Presses Universitaires de France, 1957); H. Schlier, "Die Bruderliebe nach dem Evangelium und den Briefen des Johannes," in his *Das Ende der Zeit* (Freiburg, Basel, and Vienna: Herder, 1971), pp. 124–35. On the eschatological "zeal" in Revelation, see my "Die christologischen Aussagen in den Sendschreiben der Offenbarung (Kap. 2–3)," in *Theologie aus dem Norden* (SNTU A, 2), edited by A. Fuchs (Linz: 1977), pp. 142–66.

6

The Ethos of the Bible:
Primary Constituents and
Characteristic Traits

SOME CHARACTERISTICS

By way of conclusion, I shall attempt to provide a synthetic, summary *description and characterization* of the "ethos of the Bible." In the nature of the case, a good deal of the Bible's complexity and diversity must be left out of such a picture; some of the difficulties involved were suggested in the introduction to this book. In speaking of "the Bible," I am of course referring to the Christian church's collection of holy writings, the organization of which is such that the main emphasis falls on the part presenting the "fulfillment": the writings of the *new* covenant. What follows is not intended to be a series of metaphysical or edifying statements; it is rather a brief account of the Bible's ethos, characterizing it with the help of a number of terms borrowed from later ethical thought. We begin with a rough characterization.

The ethos of the Bible has a *religious base*. It has arisen among a people over a long period of time under varying fortunes; nevertheless, a strong faith characterized this people at all times, shaping their outlook both on life in general and on the duties of humanity —those of society as well as the individual's. Fundamental to the Bible's ethos is the conviction that a disturbance in the fellowship of men and women (as within the individual) is ultimately to be explained by a disturbance in a proper relationship with God. For human beings, and for human society, to function properly and adequately, a sound relationship with God must be maintained. Moreover, the total outlook on life and the universe is determined

117

by a faith in God as all things' Creator and Sustainer. Central to the view of history is the belief that the world's present misery is a parenthesis between an original state of happiness and an ideal future which will one day be brought about by the only one who can: God. The interval between these two states is marked by the fall of humanity. It is divided into two periods. During the first, the ideal state is little more than a promise and a dim vision. The second represents a mysterious step toward the future perfection, beginning in and through a definite figure: the Son of God, Jesus Christ.

Hence God is Lord of creation in its entirety. Within creation, men and women occupy a central position, created as they are in God's image. *Humankind's* fall has the consequence that other parts of creation—the soil, plants, and animals—must suffer; and *humankind* must be restored if creation as a whole is to be "redeemed." The proper way for humankind to live involves a proper relationship with God and actions in accord with God's directions. From the biblical point of view, people themselves cannot create adequate norms for life; the Bible's ethos is not *autonomous*. But nor are the proper norms *heteronomous*: they are not imposed on men from without by an arbitrary, foreign will. According to biblical faith, the right norms for human life are *theonomous*. They come from the one who has created humankind and who is humankind's only true Lord. The demands which he makes are thus adequate and proper. When they are internalized in a person's heart, that person functions as the Creator intended, in relation both to other people and to the whole of existence.

That the Bible's ethos is theonomous does not, however, mean that God's will reaches humankind exclusively by means of special revelations from heaven (visions, holy words). In varying degrees it can also be discovered in nature (creation), in what God has done in history and in contemporary human society, in the concrete human fellowship in which one finds oneself—provided one has eyes to see and ears to hear.

The ethos of the Bible has often been described as a "character ethos" (*Gesinnungsethos*). The term may be misleading. Hellenistic philosophers, especially the Stoics, saw their ideal in the cultivating and ennobling of their personalities. And yet, their broad-mindedness notwithstanding, this ideal often led to egocentricity and a lack of concern for others. But from a biblical point of view, "my" problem cannot be solved without reference to the problem of "others" and, indeed, that of all creation. The God of the Bible is portrayed as the God of the whole universe; events and actions take place, and are intended to take place, in his world. A right relationship with him must include judicious and good efforts for the benefit of creation as a whole; a good character must be expressed and realized in good actions. On the other hand, the ethos of the Bible is not simply what is often called an "act ethos" either. The fundamental wrongs in people's behavior and fellowship cannot, according to the biblical view, be cured effectively until people are "saved" by a radical inner transformation, enabling them to live as they should. It is not enough to create favorable external conditions, to bring together fortuitous events and benevolent actions. To be sure, in a fallen world, human society is never what it ought to be; there is always a demand and a desperate need for radical improvements. But according to the biblical view, human beings themselves cannot bring about an ideal state of affairs even by the most radical revamping of society. The change must go still deeper. Human beings themselves must be transformed. The "hearts of stone" which are theirs since the fall must be replaced, by a divine act, with "hearts of flesh" (Ezek. 11:19-20; 36:26-27). Perhaps one could say that the Bible's ethos is one of primarily *inner-directed* behavior, if by this we mean a total outlook which marks all a person is and does. Nonetheless, we must remember what was just pointed out: the norms which operate in this psychic process are theonomous; further, a secondary influence from without remains part of the picture, since those who function as they should must take the demands of human fellowship and of the rest of creation into account.

This implies as well that the Bible's ethos is a *social* ethos. Fellowship is regarded as of fundamental significance for human beings. In the biblical view of things, human beings need more than health and the physical necessities of life; not even an abundance of external assets will solve more than a portion of their problems. Human beings need fellowship with others. To be abandoned and

119

lonely is regarded in the Bible as a curse, and to separate oneself in an imagined self-sufficiency is a fundamental sin. Furthermore, the Bible's ethos is anchored in the conviction that humans are *spiritual* as well as physical beings, created "in God's image" and for fellowship with him. Bread alone will not meet their needs. People's physical and material well-being may be assured while their deepest needs remain unsatisfied. Their inward being still cries in hunger and thirst for God. In other words, a definite—though not rigidly defined—view of humankind underlies the biblical ideal that the heart of stone must be replaced with one of flesh so that one can open oneself to a trusting and active fellowship with one's Creator and with others and enter into a proper relationship with the rest of creation.

In order to characterize this outlook which we find in the biblical writings the term "telos ethos" has at times been used. But even this designation seems misleading. It is true enough that biblical humanity looks forward to a *goal*; the hope of a blessed future runs throughout the Bible. But this blessed final state for the whole world is not something that humankind can achieve step by step. It is something God alone can bring about, and that at a time which he alone knows. The dimly perceived goal is often called "the reign of God," "the reign of heaven," "the Son of man's reign," "the reign of Christ," or simply "the reign." It is not, however, a clearly portrayed form of society or a defined form of government which humankind has only to create. The Bible does not provide any *simple*, explicitly *prescribed* model for politics and society, in spite of the wealth of things said about the social obligations of human beings. There is greater propriety in speaking of the New Testament's ethos for the *individual* as a kind of telos ethos, since a transformation to an increasing likeness and unity with Christ is one aspect of the course of ethical progress. But even here the term may distort. The change to likeness with Christ is not what we could call a goal in itself but rather a consequence of one's uniting with Christ in *his* self-sacrificing concern for human beings. Neither solely nor even primarily is "my" benefit the goal in view.

With this look at aspects of the general framework—primarily with a view to facilitating a comparison with ethical outlooks of other kinds—I shall now attempt to give a measure of substance to my presentation by dealing in more detail with the content and inner characteristics of the Bible's ethos.

FAITH IN THE SPIRIT OF GOD

The experience and conviction that God guides those who receive him—the "children of God"—is often expressed in the Bible with a reference to the Spirit. Those who are God's children are led by God's Spirit; that is, they are inspired to action from within by the Spirit. Biblical humanity found it natural to see the result of the Spirit's ministry in all good qualities and actions, but particularly in those which were in some way extraordinary.

For Moses, it was a glorious ideal that all God's people might receive the Lord's Spirit in fullest measure, so that all of them would become prophets (Num. 11:29). One consequence of this view of the Spirit was the Old Testament expectation that the coming ideal time of salvation would be characterized by the Spirit, which would then be richly poured out over God's people (especially Joel 2:28–29). There are links with these expectations in the New Testament, both in the depiction of Jesus as the one who has the Spirit in full measure and in the fact that the people of the new covenant (the "Israel according to the Spirit") see themselves as the possessors of God's Spirit. Throughout the New Testament we meet the conviction that the Spirit is present and active among those who are rightly related to God. Still it is of interest to note that the theme is treated by the different authors in differing ways. They do not all reckon equally with the Spirit's activity as a factor when they account for human behavior as it should be. The Spirit's role is strongly emphasized by Luke, John, and Paul. Paul can summarize the new relationship with God which has been established "in Christ" as "walking in the Spirit." He depicts the Spirit's work as sovereign and "fruit"-yielding. But in the Epistle of James the Spirit is mentioned but once at the most (4:5, but the reference is not clear). And for Matthew, Jesus is, to be sure, filled with the Spirit, and all that he does is done in the Spirit's power, but when obedience to the will of God is defined and described, the Spirit is not so much as mentioned.

Thus the New Testament authors all believe that the proper ethos can become a reality only when God's power inspires a person

121

from within, but they describe the matter in different ways. Even when speaking of such a fundamental factor as the Spirit, their language is different.

LOVE

Part of the biblical vision is the picture of *familia Dei*: God is the heavenly Father, and those who worship him are his children, "the family of God." It is natural for relations within the ideal fellowship of this vision to be designated with the word "love" (*ahavah, agapē*), a word which expresses not only a feeling but a total attitude. The significance of the word does shift somewhat between its use for the father's love of his children and the children's of their father. The Old Testament contains many beautiful descriptions of God's love as a father for his people: "I have dearly loved you from of old, and still I maintain my unfailing care for you" (Jer. 31:3 NEB). Israel's duty to love God is also stressed.

The motif of "sacred familial love" is the subject of increasingly profound treatment—especially in certain circles—within Judaism of the postexilic period, but it is involved in an uphill struggle with other trends. During this period, the people of Israel are consolidated into a theocracy in which God's will is law. Furthermore, the threat of annihilation from without compels Jews to defend their holy law with life and blood. Under the pressure of bitter circumstances, the will of the heavenly Father comes to be conceived as commands and statutes which must be loyally and carefully kept. Love for God takes the form of scrupulous observance of a detailed network of regulations about right and wrong, clean and unclean, permitted and forbidden. The will of God is interpreted in a more statutory way than before.

It is very typical of the transformation wrought by Jesus that the relationship with God loses its association with a "state" and its character of being regulated by statutes, becoming instead an immediate family relationship. And naturally enough, this makes love the focus of attention. "Love" serves as a summarizing term for the proper ethos toward God and humankind. But here too we find diversity in the thinking and terminology of the various New Testament books. The Johannine writings are marked by a profound reflection on the problems of what constitutes the proper life and how such a life comes about. Here ethical thinking is concentrated entirely on the question of *love's* mystery, the secrets of "God-love." No concrete ethical questions are taken up for discussion. In the Pauline Letters, the conviction is expressed in a number of ways that love is the crucial element in a proper way of living; all good words and actions are futile unless they are borne by love (1 Corinthians 13!). Moreover, the principle which governs love is worked out in a clear way: love is the giving of oneself, a self-sacrifice in obedience to the will of God and for the benefit of others. In Matthew's Gospel we see that the word *agapē* can for the most part be omitted—though the corresponding verb is used in crucial texts —and replaced with other words ("righteousness," "to hear and do the word," "to do the will of the Father in heaven," "to be merciful toward" or "to show compassion for" one's fellows) without upsetting love's position as the fundamental principle in a proper way of life.

When a right attitude toward God and humankind is understood in such a direct fashion, it naturally follows that quantities of commands, and particularly regulations of ritual and rules of observance, become submerged or are directly abolished. A further characteristic is that the two commands of love for God (Deut. 6:5) and love for one's neighbor (Lev. 19:18) are combined, at times even to the extent that duties toward one's fellows are presented as all that is required (for example, in the golden rule). This extremely important feature in the Bible's ethos must be allowed its full weight, especially when biblical ethics are compared with other ethical systems. But if this feature is treated by itself in isolation, and only maxims of this type are cited out of the abundance of relevant texts, then fundamental aspects of the biblical outlook go unnoticed. The basic conviction that an adequate and complete relation with one's fellow human beings is only possible when the relation with God has become what it should is then neglected. In the process, one loses sight of what in the Bible is presented as humanity's greatest and—in the final analysis—only indispensable good: *God* himself. Humans, according to biblical faith, are not at the mercy of things corruptible: either of other humans (who may disappoint and fail) or of creation's blessings (which may be lost or never come at all). They have, above the transient world, a point unmoved, imparting to life an incomparable sustaining power. In the midst of ruins, deprivation, and anguish, they can say to their God, "Having thee, I desire nothing else on earth" (Ps. 73:25 NEB).

Only in exceptional cases does Paul use the word "love" of the ideal relationship with God. Primarily he speaks instead of "faith" (*pistis*). But he too keeps the two aspects together. Faith—when it is living—is "active in love." Faith of necessity yields "fruit" for the benefit of others. This is so obvious to the "apostle of faith" that he can without hesitation declare love greater than faith itself (1 Corinthians 13).

That love is a mysterious gift from God, received when the Spirit has been allowed to waken a response in an open and willing heart, has been expressed not least by Paul: "God's love has been poured into our hearts through the Holy Spirit which has been given to us" (Rom. 5:5 RSV).

THE IMITATION AND PRESENCE
OF CHRIST

A further feature must be noted in a characterization of the New Testament's ethos: it bears the stamp of *Christ*, though in varying ways and degrees.

1. In the Letter of James, Jesus is not presented as a model. In fact he is only mentioned twice. Nonetheless, the ethical admonition here given has strong links with the teaching of Jesus, and in particular with the Sermon on the Mount. The ethos of the Epistle bears the stamp of Christ in the sense that its content and spirit are determined by the message of Jesus.

2. In the other books of the New Testament—with the exception of 3 John and Jude—the stamp of Christ has penetrated more deeply and become of the essence of the ethos we encounter. Jesus is regarded as the ideal human being who himself embodies the right way to live. The early Christian teachers and preachers saw in Jesus so perfect a representative of the ideal way of living that they could present their ethical program in epic form by simply telling about him. That they identify Jesus Christ and "love" is evident in a number of ways. In the Gospel of Matthew, for example, we see how the evangelist goes to great trouble to illustrate what the two love commands require. This he does in part by relating what Jesus

taught in word, but also by stylizing his whole narrative about Jesus' character and behavior in such a way that the patterns of his way of life (his "love") will stand out as clearly as possible. John says quite explicitly that "we" have learned what love is by Christ's sacrifice of his life for us, and that we are under obligation to walk as he walked and love one another as he has loved us. Paul speaks of a love which does not "look to its own interests, but to the interests of others," then portrays Christ as the example whom all should follow.

When the New Testament's ethos is thus presented as an imitation of Christ, the same psychic mechanisms are set in motion as function when any figure is made a person's ideal ("idol"). A process of imitation, an "identification," takes place on a very elementary plane. The spreading of an ethos which is conveyed in this way—especially when it is done by a whole group acknowledging the same ideal figure—is in part a subconscious process. We are here dealing with an ethos which is very little intellectualized. Here the childlike, undeveloped mind (the "simple") has no more difficulty—perhaps even less—in keeping pace and assimilating than the mature and sophisticated has. There is ample evidence that early Christianity's ethos was from the first effective with the "simple and unlearned" as well as with others. To the great benefit of posterity, the evangelists chose to convey the Bible's ethos in this elementary and vital way by preserving the narratives about Jesus—and quite rightly, the church has placed the texts of the Gospels in the foreground of its teaching. Much of this simple and extremely effective method of communicating the "attitude of Christ" is lost if Christian preaching and teaching become one-sidedly doctrinal in character.

3. The stamp of Christ achieves its full depth, however, only when the imitation of Christ is accompanied by the conviction of his presence. For the people of the New Testament, Christ was not simply the subject of narratives from the past, a memory on which to reflect and by which to be instructed. Christ was the living Lord; in prayer, in worship services, and in the struggle for faith and proper living, his existence and presence were felt. The teachers of early Christianity unhesitatingly distinguished between other model figures whom they recognized and whose image they bore in their

"hearts" (Abraham, Isaac, the prophets, the martyrs, and so forth) and the Christ who himself had "taken up residence" in the "hearts" of his followers, who was "indwelling" them. In their work for the cause of Jesus, and especially in times of difficulty and suffering, Christians experienced the presence of their heavenly Commissioner. Paul speaks in a number of places of the fellowship he enjoys with Christ at the very time he suffers as an apostle of Jesus Christ; the presence of "the Lord" provides the comfort and strength needed to endure it all. John too speaks repeatedly of the mysterious personal fellowship between the risen Lord and his followers and disciples: he "abides" in them and they "abide" in him. The ancient notions of God's "presence" in the midst of his people, and of the Spirit's resting upon those chosen of God, have thus been intensified and personalized. Christ is the one who is near. His presence means forgiveness, inspiration, and spiritual strength but is itself something more than that. Unless this element in the New Testament's ethos is considered, its profound uniqueness is not done justice.

WORLD AFFIRMATION AND SACRIFICE

The love of which the Bible speaks is essentially a giving of oneself, a willingness to sacrifice. One is to give generously of oneself, to share what one has, even—if God so demands—to sacrifice everything, including one's life. In certain respects a similar outlook is found in Stoicism. There, however, it is a matter of raising oneself above all things earthly: such things are regarded as of no relevance or worth, and the task of the wise is to free their minds of them. The biblical view, in its classical form, does not link the demand to sacrifice with such a despising of the world. Rather, from the very beginning it is part of a vision markedly affirmative toward life: sacrifice is demanded so that life may go on and more fruit be borne.

According to biblical faith, the world in its entirety is created by God and thus *good* (compare the Creation narrative with which the Bible begins). There is, however, a reservation: the world has been perverted (the story of humanity's fall). This reservation can be developed so strongly that an outlook which renounces the world is the result. Of the biblical writings, it is the Johannine that go furthest in this direction. Here the view is almost dualistic, though typically enough it is not wholly so; even here it is fundamental that God has created everything and that he in the end will restore the world from its fall. Evil is recognized as a fearful reality, a destructive factor constantly active in God's created world. At times it is even said that the world is in the power of the evil one. But evil is not regarded as a wholly independent force. This is most apparent in visions of the future. That God in the end will achieve his good purposes is never questioned.

It is true that world-renouncing attitudes and statements can be found in many places in the Bible. These tendencies have broadened into a generally pessimistic world view in Ecclesiastes. In the Johannine writings, they have led to an almost dualistic outlook with the slogan "Love not the world!" They are an important element in the strongly eschatological outlook and expectations of many New Testament books. In Paul the marked concentration on eschatology has led to an attitude almost Stoic in its exaltation above all that the present age can offer. Nonetheless, the fact remains that the dominating, fundamental view in the Bible is clearly positive toward life in the world which God has created.

The task of loving God "with your whole heart" (Deut. 6:5) thus does not mean that one is to turn one's back on the world and on life in it. It means that one is to live according to the will of God amid the conditions of earthly life—to be "*in* the world but not *of* the world," as John puts it. The needs and functions of the body are not, in the biblical view, something evil which ought to be done away with, or something worthless to which no attention should be paid. To be sure, the body is part of the corruptible world. But it too is a divine creation and the object of a divine redemptive concern. When, in the course of the centuries during which the Bible was written, faith in a resurrection becomes developed, the body characteristically is given a place in the world to come, though admittedly in a "glorified" form. The body is, however, humanity's Achilles' heel. Whether it is said that "the flesh is weak" (that is, humanity's weak point) or that "the flesh is at war with the Spirit" (that is, that it is strong, and opposes the will of God), the body is regarded as fertile soil for sin in a person and a classic point of the tempter's attack. When he wants to entice humans to act against God's will, both the weakness of the body and the strong desires of the "flesh" (with their center in the "heart") draw his attention. The body's desires must therefore be disciplined into yielding obedience to God. They need not be put to death. But many severe formulations—especially in Paul—witness how seriously the struggle against the animal impulses within a person was taken. Hence the basic demand that God's children *love him with their whole heart*, that is, with a "heart" neither hardened nor divided (by lust).

In the Bible, one's greatest earthly possession is seen as life itself; "all that a man has he will give for his life." Humankind's love of life is both assumed and affirmed. The life of a human being is not to be taken. The Preacher may speak about life in this world with skepticism and contempt. Paul may say that he would rather depart than remain in this earthly life. But even for these two, the basic view that life is precious and inviolable remains unshaken. In the biblical view of things, one does not have the right to take other people's or one's own life, not even in the disguised form of bringing about one's own martyrdom when the situation does not demand it. Jesus tells his disciples to be on their watch and to take advantage of opportunities to flee in times of persecution—as long as this does not involve denying faith or other disastrous results. He himself avoids his mortal foes until the time when God requires that he give himself into their hand. In Gethsemane he prays that, *if possible*, he may avoid a premature, violent death.

For those who love life and long to retain it, death is a fearful evil. The Bible takes this evil seriously. The dread of physical death is regarded—realistically enough—as one of the gravest of threats to a person's obedience towards God. At death's door, even the best of people are tempted to preserve their lives at any cost. In this situation all other values—including that of obeying God's will—are in danger of being set aside. Here lies another of the tempter's classical points of attack, and a special reminder is needed: You shall love the Lord your God *with your whole soul* (that is, even if it costs you life itself). Martyrdom in order to hold fast to God's will, and thereby also promote the good of humanity, is regarded as a sacrifice—a sacrifice of the same mysterious sort as the death of the grain of wheat in the soil for the sake of what will grow and bear fruit in its season. Hence it benefits others. Further, those who so sacrifice themselves pass on to a new and higher life: "He who

loses his life [here on earth] for my sake will find it [in eternity]"
(RSV). In times of martyrdom, then, this transient life and that of
eternity confront each other, and priority is given to eternity's.

Humankind's resources other than life and the body are designated with the late Hebrew word *mamon* (in English, traditionally
"mammon"). The term covers both material possessions and the
status and power associated with wealth. Wealth is part of what
the Bible calls "(divine) blessing." Poverty is almost always regarded as a situation involving great need. Even where it is embraced as an ideal, the poor are presented as needy and vulnerable
so that others will provide them with their basic requirements. But
here too human appreciation of what in itself is recognized as of
value constitutes a threat. Throughout the Bible runs the theme
that human beings at this point, in their relation to mammon, are
wide open for the temptation to set their hearts on something other
than God, thereby neglecting God's will and falling away from
him. In the biblical view, the love of and unrestrained striving for
power and wealth are nothing other than idolatry. "You cannot
serve God and mammon."

In the New Testament, an attitude of watchfulness and distrust
toward riches is generally enjoined. Paul's attitude, as we have already suggested, reminds of Stoic *autarkeia*. Property and earthly
status are for him things indifferent; one can do equally well with
or without them. Since his guiding principle is to give of himself, to
sacrifice himself for the good of others, this means that he abstains
from whatever is not indispensable to his task. Luke—who shows
great interest in the problem of "the rich and the poor"—has poverty as an ideal. This is true too of the author of James. Matthew
views the matter chiefly as a question of one's willingness to make
sacrifices for the sake of the reign of heaven. For him the rule is,
the greater the sacrifice, the greater the "reward." But in spite of
such variations, the view is shared by all that wealth and power
among human beings—precisely because they are values human
beings hold high—represent one of the most serious threats to
human obedience to God. "The love of money is the root of all
evils." It is no coincidence that it is stressed that love for God must
be a love *with your whole strength* (that is, it is to rule even one's
attitude toward power and possessions).

These brief outlines of a few fundamental convictions and values held by the people of the Bible have been sketched as a reminder of the positive background to the biblical view of sacrifice. The picture is clear: life in this world is not in itself sinful. Humans are not required to despise it or show indifference toward it. The requirement is rather that it be placed at the service of the God who gives life. One must be able to make sacrifices, to sacrifice oneself, even to sacrifice one's most treasured possession, should God so desire and the good of humanity so require. Hence this too is a demand for an open, obedient, and loving heart. No involvement of the "heart" is needed to sacrifice what one despises or holds indifferent. But when what one holds dear is offered, a proof of love from the "heart" is given.

GIFT AND DEMAND

It is axiomatic for the biblical outlook that God's initiative and action precede human beings'. This is true of creation, election, salvation, and ultimate redemption. Humankind's love for God is in fact roused by God himself—indeed, it is bestowed by God as a gift. It has the character of a response. "We love because he first loved us" is a New Testament statement, but it could equally well have stood in the Old Testament (see, for example, Deut. 10:14–16). In the New Testament this insight is concentrated on one point above all others. Return is repeatedly made to the fact that Christ—as God's representative and in accordance with God's will—gave himself to a violent death for the sake of those who rejected him, betrayed him—or did not know about him.

It is characteristic of the ethos we meet in the New Testament that the ethical ideals it sets are extremely high. God's demands are unlimited, boundless: he desires to have a person in entirety; he demands everything. If this were the whole truth about the outlook which emerges from the New Testament, there would be good cause for calling the divine demands unreasonable "over-demands." But in fact this is only one element of a total picture in which God's own work is strongly emphasized. God is active in us, creating in us both the desire and the ability to do what we should. He impels human beings by his Spirit. Christ is present with his inspiration and power. And divine grace comes first as well as last; it precedes a person's ethical endeavors, sustains them throughout, and envelops them with its forgiveness.

In earlier chapters I have attempted to show how three of early Christianity's greatest teachers communicate the New Testament vision and the ethos which is a part of it. Their views show profound agreement, and the ethos they represent is in many ways similar. There is, however, a difference between Matthew and Paul which should be mentioned here. Paul maintains with unparalleled radicalism as the basis of the whole Christian message the fact "that Christ died for our sins in accordance with the scriptures, that he was buried, that he was raised on the third day in accordance with the scriptures" (RSV), and that thereby a new foundation for life has been laid—and laid by God. Here is worked out with clarity and emphasis a fundamental principle found throughout early Christianity: Christ is not simply a model; he has accomplished something on which all others are dependent and must build; his work is the basis on which the Christian ethos must be established. For Paul one fact must be given priority over everything else: all are guilty before God; none passes the test of God's gaze in judgment; but God now gives the world the opportunity to begin anew, making a sovereign and conditionless offer of salvation and eternal life for Christ's sake—just as it is God who sovereignly brings salvation to its completion by working "in you, both to will and to work for his good pleasure" (Phil. 2:12–13 RSV).

Matthew, for his part, also shows in many ways that God's grace and Christ's death ("for the forgiveness of sins," "as a ransom for many") are a firm foundation on which all must fall back. Even the foremost person of the church, Peter, is condemned unless his Lord grants him forgiveness (10:33; 26:69–75). But Matthew has not drawn equally radical consequences as Paul has from the fact of Messiah's sacrifice. It is characteristic of Matthew that he places decisive importance on works of love. In his view, those whose lives are marked by deeds of mercy toward their fellows will meet the standard on the day of judgment.

Paul too contends that works of love will be decisive at the final judgment—at least for the more nuanced distribution of "rewards" and "punishments." But for him such works are only the inevitable consequences of faith in the gospel of Christ and the Spirit's ministry in the heart. "The fruit of the Spirit" is what is sought from human beings at the judgment. Should it be lacking, all is lacking. In Paul's view, Christ by his death has put an end to the law's rule.

God now guides his "family" in the world by different means. For those who are "in Christ," there simply is no divine law. Hence there are no binding obligations and, as a result, no "debts," no guilt. The insight that Christ by his death has done away both with humankind's *debts* and with their prerequisite, the *law*, has been allowed to make a clean sweep. The old order has passed away. In the new situation which has been created, the "children of God" have the right to feel themselves free of debt toward God. They serve God, but in freely offered love, inspired by the Spirit.

Matthew for his part has very deliberately and clearly shown that even the leaders of the church must live by forgiveness. The eleven who encounter the risen Lord on a mountain in Galilee (Matthew 28) have, by deserting Christ, forfeited their right to represent him. If they now nonetheless are sent out on Christ's mission, it is because they have been pardoned and received back into favor. The conditions of their commissioning are different from what they were when the disciples were first sent out (chapter 10). But for Matthew, the law remains in force. Jesus has fulfilled it, but it is still valid. The relationship has been sublimated, but humankind still stands under sacred demands—and very high ones at that. Hence the possibility of accumulating debts remains; so too that of accumulating "rewards," treasures in heaven. Matthew has undoubtedly been very faithful to the Jesus tradition at his disposal. But he has not viewed it with that perspective of distance which Paul enjoyed. Morever, he is tied in his book to the concrete material before him, that of the traditions about Jesus' earthly ministry. Paul, by way of contrast, composes his own letters and is free to choose both subject matter and substance. What hinders Matthew is not felt by Paul when he develops the consequences of the decisive elements of the basic kerygma about Christ's redemptive work.

Perhaps the historical and psychological side of the matter is that Matthew was one of those scribes who were "trained for the reign of heaven" (13:52). In his case, instruction, discussion, and personal reflection had gradually brought clarity (*synienai*). Paul, on the other hand, was a scribe who was suddenly given a vision of the risen Lord at the very time he was engaged in persecuting Jesus' cause; that vision created faith (*pistis*) in him and made him an apostle of Jesus Christ (Galatians 1). This was the starting point from which he was compelled to rethink things radically. And he proved to be one who could do it.

FELLOWSHIP AND DISTANCE

It is natural that an ethos as fellowship-oriented as that of the Bible is maintained not by isolated individuals but by a community: Israel, or "Israel according to the Spirit" (the church). Throughout the Bible runs the notion of a people of God, though it assumes different forms and is given varying degrees of emphasis. God is represented in the world by a chosen "people." The problems related with the institutional side of this theme (institutions, offices, and so on) are important ones, but ones which I felt could be omitted in this study. Several problems of particular ethical concern should, however, be touched upon.

The fellowship of the people of God, with its center in community worship, represents the soil in which the individual is to grow. Within this primary fellowship, the views, values, ideals, and attitudes to which the common faith gives birth are nurtured. The members can support each other. The value of complete unity (and of equality in the eyes of the Creator) is emphasized in the Bible, but there is also an underlining of the benefits which *differences* can bring when they are handled properly; that is, when the various gifts are all used for the good of the fellowship as a whole. The duties of those who are "strong" (in various respects) toward "the weak" are stressed throughout the Bible. The underlying principle is that greater gifts bring greater responsibilities. The duty of providing help for those less privileged (in whatever way) finds a number of memorable expressions: one is to be "eyes for the blind and feet for the lame," and so forth. Paul has sketched the various roles which different people must play in the common fellowship with a sure hand: in his picture of the body with its many different parts, all serving the common good; and in his insistence that the various gifts of the Spirit have been distributed in order that they may accomplish something *together*. What he says about different parts of the body is misused if it is cited in order to squelch efforts intended to do away with injustices that can in fact be dealt with. Jesus' self-sacrificing followers ought, in the New Testament view, to be in the vanguard where such efforts are made, themselves

133

setting an example. Nonetheless, the statements of a duty to serve one another and the fellowship as a whole on the very basis of a difference in gifts cannot be *replaced* by any thought of equality so long as people differ in their physical and spiritual equipment. The slogan "We are all members, for the benefit of one another" is one of those mottoes as meaningful in today's fellowship life as ever.

There are many aspects to the biblical notion of the people of God. The vision of the chosen people as a "kingdom of priests and a holy nation" combines elements which can be accentuated in different ways. One can focus on the thought of holiness. The primary task then becomes that of making oneself holy, of separating oneself ritually and by a holy praxis from the heathen and their ways. Or the thought of sacrifice may be stressed. The task of God's people is then the one indicated in the songs of "the Lord's servant" (*eved Jahwe*): to offer themselves for the good of the world. Both thoughts are developed in postexilic Judaism. We have seen how close the classical interpretation given to Israel's "confession of faith" (the *Shema*) comes to the basic idea found in the songs of the Lord's suffering servant. But in the course of difficult centuries, and particularly during the cultural struggle which began in the days of the Maccabees, the former thought (that of holiness) got the upper hand.

It is characteristic of Jesus that he radicalizes the notion that the children of God are to be "the Lord's servants" and to sacrifice themselves for others: the individual for the fellowship, and the people of God for the world. The cultivation of this idea of love means that the ideal of holiness must give way. In the process, walls are torn down. Doors are opened to the unholy and unclean, to sinners and heathen. In the Gospels, we see how Jesus by his actions sets aside the current prescriptions of ritual which would have kept him from reaching "the lost" and in his teaching speaks of a love which is to include all, including foes and persecutors. And we see from early Christianity's reworking of the Jesus traditions that his attitude toward "tax collectors and prostitutes" was adopted as a model for the young church's attitude toward the "Gentiles."

This fellowship of love which breaks through the boundaries prescribed by holiness has been understood and given expression by Matthew in his Gospel. But the synoptic evangelist to give it greatest emphasis is Luke. For Paul, the wall has been broken down (Ephesians 2!); the idea that the gospel is for sinners is—as we have seen—developed by him with unequaled clarity. Even such a writing as the Epistle of James keeps the boundaries open. (Here I do not discuss the struggle which early Christianity waged for clarity in all the complicated questions arising when fellowship with "Gentiles" was put into practice.)

In the Johannine writings, however, Jesus' teaching of a duty to love outsiders and sinners has not been preserved. Jesus' new commandment in John's version is that Christians are to love *one another* as Jesus has loved them. The insights that love is a gift from God and that it involves a complete sacrifice are maintained without diminution: "we ought to lay down our lives for the brethren." But one boundary has returned: the demarcation demanded by holiness to the exclusion of outsiders, "the world." It is clear enough why this is so. Within the churches, false teachers sow discord. Against this threat John directs his fervent admonition for harmony and for genuine love which bears the brand of Jesus. Further, the Christians —who here see themselves as children of light in a world of darkness—are a small, badgered, and beleaguered lot. Evidently it is a time of persecution. The darkness outside their own ranks is much too fearful, the hatred and threats they feel from without much too strong for the children of light to show love toward all. Admittedly, the right to hate outsiders is not here given (as it was in the Qumran sect). But neither is there any word enjoining a love which embraces all—including "the children of the world," enemies and persecutors. The breadth of Jesus' vision of love has not been preserved.

We have reason to note two things here. First, an experience with which Jews were familiar even before Christ: the right way of living certainly creates fellowship, but it also creates *one* kind of division. It draws forth a peculiar hatred from those who stubbornly resist it. This hatred does not come only from the "heathen." It comes also—and in a form of great intensity—from certain representatives of "the people of God." "It cannot be that a prophet should perish away from Jerusalem!" (RSV, emphasis added). Second, persecution from without is one of those factors which easily can bring about a perversion of the ideal represented by the

Bible's ethos. In both Jewish (the Dead Sea Scrolls, the Books of the Maccabees) and early Christian writings (the Johannine books) there appear symptoms typical of times of persecution: not only a strengthening of the fellowship within the people of God, but also a walling in, a defensiveness, and a curtailed love. Part of Jesus' program according to the synoptic tradition is that love is to be maintained and self-sacrificing action to be carried out even in times of martyrdom. Even when darkness falls on all sides, generous, sacrificial, vulnerable love is to continue.

Paul has—often in inspired, hymnic form—portrayed this exalted attitude in the midst of a world where others do differently. Jesus' theme is here preserved in a vital, independent way. We have already quoted some of the passages in which the apostle describes the ideal life style which, positively, is true to its own program without being contaminated and confused by the methods of its environment. According to Paul, a right relation with God creates an inner freedom which is complete (except, of course, for its ties to Christ). Against this inner liberty and independence external circumstances contend to no avail. Nothing can entice it from its course; nothing can shake it from its foundation; nothing, ultimately, has significance in comparison with it.

We do, however, note a dilemma in Paul. When the concept of love is combined—as it is in Paul—with a strong sense of eschatological expectation, the threat of curtailment comes from a different direction. The expectation of the coming age's glories may be so strong that the Christian begins to cut his ties already from the world in which his obligations are to be fulfilled. Paul's outlook— which may be influenced somewhat by Stoic ideals—retains some reservations about entering into fellowship. It is marked by a certain distance with respect not only to this age whose end is approaching, but also to one's fellows. When Paul goes so far as to say that those who are married should live as though they were not, we see that his ideal can lead to an inner reservation toward others which even includes one's wife or husband. Such a reservation is scarcely congruous with the principle that love for one's fellows is to take the form of wholehearted compassion, an acceptance of responsibility toward others, and a full sharing in their sufferings.

The synoptic Gospels present us with a somewhat different picture on this point. Jesus Christ is there depicted as one who himself assumes the miseries of human beings and shares in their needs; and he does this with no inner reservations and without deriving strength from a premature breaking of ties with this world. Here too the sacrifice of his own life is portrayed as an act of obedience done amid great anguish. The distinction I am drawing becomes apparent if, for example, the synoptic narrative of Jesus in Gethsemane is compared with Paul's description of his own attitude in Phil. 1:20-26.

The ideal of self-sacrifice also stamps the biblical view of the church's task toward the world around it. The early Christian message bearers did not go out into their Hellenistic environs in order to win something for themselves, to accrue benefits themselves at the cost of a dying world. The task of the church in their view was to missionize and give of itself in order that the world might be saved. Before the rulers of this age, the church was not to demand privileges but to "witness for the truth"—and suffer the consequences. The attitude they held toward those in positions of political authority, as well as the obligations they felt within society in general, were sketched above at the ends of chapters two and four. What was said there need not be repeated here.

A couple of final observations should be made with regard to the question how the Bible's ethos relates to the insights and ethos of men in general. In Acts and above all in the Pauline Letters we can see what nature the encounter took on between early Christianity's ethos and the ethical values embraced by the Hellenistic world. We note that Paul is able to conduct a debate with outsiders on ethical questions. This is partly because he has a strong, clear vision of God's purposes and man's needs, and partly because he is able to assess individual qualities and actions and judge them as good or evil. By means of the breadth of his experience and knowledge, the apostle is able to discover points of common value and to clarify and make use of a fact not easily grasped: that the apparently unique and exclusive Christian proclamation has profound points of contact with the general ethical values of humankind. Actually, it is hardly surprising that Paul, with his strong conviction that God is Lord both of creation and of history, was able to perceive traces of the divine Lordship even outside the boundaries of Israel and the church.

HUMANITY'S DUTIES TOWARD THE
REST OF CREATION

The ethical obligations of humanity go beyond those to God and other human beings. The God of the Bible stands in relation to creation in its entirety. He is everything's Source and Sovereign, and he is responsible for everything. He "rejoices in his works" and cares for them; "his compassion is over all that he has made." These are not simply poetic formulations found in prophetic utterances and hymns; they express an important element in what is fundamental to faith in "the Lord of heaven and earth."

Humankind's important position on earth as God's governor is indicated in a number of ways. Their original fall has brought with it a curse upon the soil. When God's people time and again draw punishment upon themselves, the land—its soil, plants, and animals—suffers as well. Consistent with this notion is the depiction of the blessings of the coming salvation as affecting not only humanity but the rest of the earth as well. Paul speaks of all creation as eagerly awaiting the glorious deliverance of the children of God (Romans 8). Early Christianity's vision of the future links up with ancient prophecies as well as with sayings of Jesus in its expectation of the coming of "new heavens and a new earth in which righteousness dwells" (2 Pet. 3:13 RSV).

Humankind's position as God's governor on earth means that humans are permitted to rule the animals, use the plants to meet their physical needs, and exploit the soil. But it does not give them free reign for unrestrained self-will and heedless tyranny. Obligations accompany the position of power and the resources they have received. To whom much is given, of them much will be required. If they are to fulfill their role as the image and representative of God on earth, then they—like God—are to rejoice in God's work and rule over it but also to take responsibility for it, and to show compassion for everything entrusted and subordinated to them: animals, plants, matter. Humanity's responsibility toward the rest of creation thus has its base in the view of God as Creator and humankind as his representative—or, put more broadly, in the Bible's view of God and humankind.

THE FUNDAMENTAL SIN

In this description and characterization of the Bible's ethos I have not focused attention on the *opposite* of right living—sin, faithlessness, defeat—but contented myself with a sketch of the positive basis of a right way of living. By way of conclusion, however, I must briefly mention the *fundamental* sin as it is portrayed in the Bible. The opposite of the "love" which is the ideal attitude in life (Deut. 6:5) is defined in the Bible in many different ways, in such formulations as, for example, to "harden one's heart," "live for oneself," "look to one's own interests." What is meant is egoism: withholding one's "heart" from God and other people, regarding life as one's own possession, grabbing for oneself instead of giving to others.

Throughout the Bible, perceptive people of God track down the various forms which such an attitude takes. Here may be placed the never-ceasing criticism of religious institutionalization and routinization: sacrifice with no will for it, circumcision that leaves the heart uncircumcised, fasting without repentance, knowledge of God's law without the fear of God, almsgiving designed to increase one's own esteem, prayer without the heart's devotion, scrupulous observance of rules governing tithe of mint and dill and cummin while the central commands of the heart are neglected, faith without the works of the heart, the sacrificing of all one has without love in the heart. Paul has perceived that even martyrdom can be a means to seek one's own ends (1 Cor. 13:3).

The purpose of this unending struggle is not a simple matter of abolishing all institutions, rituals, and routinized patterns of behavior. The point of the critique is not that such things are evil and ought to be avoided. There is a double emphasis. First, that institutions can in fact function, rituals be performed, and ethical programs be carried out while the heart is not giving of itself in fellowship with God and others. Behind the façade and the routines, the center of the personality may very well remain unengaged, free to pursue its own interests. The heart is still closed to God; he is not permitted to rouse a living love or to inspire living deeds. Second, that institutions of religion, words of piety, and acts of holiness can in fact be used as the subtlest of shelters *against* God (and thereby also against one's fellows). It is precisely these sacred things that appear to be what God requires and what—if anything—will serve to satisfy him; they seem to provide both what he demands and additional merits besides, thus affording one security and self-sufficiency even in the presence of *God*. The religious apparatus can be used as a sophisticated tool to free one of one's dependency on God and others; rebellion against God is often disguised in holy garb.

The continual flight of the human heart from God takes its toll on other human beings as well (and on animals, plants, and the soil). This thought is repeatedly expressed. When the Bible's prophets and teachers summon "God's children" back to order, they point as a rule to those symptoms which are apparent in interhuman relationships. The lack of love seen there reflects a lack of love toward God. John's First Epistle puts it succinctly: "He who does not love does not know God; for God is love" (RSV).

Bibliography

At the close of each chapter, a few special studies have been mentioned. Here are listed a number of summary works as well as others on limited questions important to our subject which do not restrict themselves too narrowly to one particular part of the Bible. The list deals with monographs only.

GENERAL

Agrell, G. *Work, Toil and Sustenance: An Examination of the View of Work in the New Testament, Taking into Consideration Views Found in the Old Testament, Intertestamental and Early Rabbinic Writings.* Lund: H. Ohlsson, 1976.

Bultmann, Rudolf. *Theology of the New Testament.* 2 vols. New York: Charles Scribner's Sons, 1951–55; London: SCM Press, 1952–55.

Dewar, L. *An Outline of New Testament Ethics.* Philadelphia: Westminster Press, 1949.

Dihle, A. *Die goldene Regel: Eine Einführung in die Geschichte der antiken und frühchristlichen Vulgärethik.* Göttingen: Vandenhoeck & Ruprecht, 1962.

Dodd, C. H. *Gospel and Law.* New York: Columbia University Press, 1951.

Forkman, G. *The Limits of the Religious Community: Expulsion from the Religious Community Within the Qumran Sect, Within Rabbinic Judaism, and Within Primitive Christianity.* Lund: C. W. K. Gleerup, 1972.

Grant, F. C. *The Economic Background of the Gospels.* London: Oxford University Press, 1926.

Grant, R. M. *Early Christianity and Society.* New York: Harper & Row, Publishers, 1977.

Greeven, H. *Das Hauptproblem der Sozialethik in der neueren Stoa und im Urchristentum.* Gütersloh: C. Bertelsmann, 1935.

Hempel, J. *Das Ethos des Alten Testaments.* Berlin: Töpelmann, 1938.

Hengel, M. *Property and Riches in the Early Church: Aspects of a*

Social History of Early Christianity. Philadelphia: Fortress Press, 1974; London: SCM Press, 1974.

Houlden, J. L. *Ethics and the New Testament.* Harmondsworth, England: Penguin Books, 1973.

Lagrange, M. J. *La morale de l'évangile: Réflections sur "les morales de l'évangile" de M. A. Bayet.* 2d ed. Paris: Grasset, 1931.

Leipoldt, J. *Der soziale Gedanke in der altchristlichen Kirche.* Leipzig: Koehler & Amelang, 1952.

Lohmeyer, E. *Soziale Fragen im Urchristentum.* Leipzig: Quelle & Meyer, 1921.

Manson, T. W. *Ethics and Gospel.* New York: Charles Scribner's Sons, 1960.

Marshall, L. H. *The Challenge of New Testament Ethics.* London: Macmillan, 1946.

Mealand, D. L. *Poverty and Expectation in the Gospels.* London, 1979.

Nielsen, E. *The Ten Commandments in New Perspective: A Traditio-Historical Approach.* Naperville, Ill.: Alec R. Allenson, 1968.

Noll, P. *Jesus und das Gesetz.* Tübingen: Mohr, 1968.

Osborn, E. F. *Ethical Patterns in Early Christian Thought.* Cambridge: University Press, 1976.

Oyen, H. van. *Ethik des Alten Testaments.* Gütersloh: G. Mohn, 1967.

Piper, J. *"Love Your Enemies": Jesus' Love Command in the Synoptic Gospels and the Early Christian Paraenesis.* Cambridge: University Press, 1979.

Richter, W. *Recht und Ethos: Versuch einer Ortung des weisheitlichen Mahnspruches.* Munich: Kösel-Verlag, 1966.

Schelkle, K. H. *Theology of the New Testament.* Collegeville, Minn.: Liturgical Press, 1971– .

Schlatter, A. *Die christliche Ethik.* Stuttgart: Calwer, 1914.

Schnackenburg, R. *The Moral Teaching of the New Testament.* London: Burns & Oates, 1975.

Schottroff, L., and Stegemann, W. *Jesus von Nazareth—Hoffnung der Armen.* Stuttgart: Kohlhammer, 1978.

Spicq, C. *Théologie morale du Nouveau Testament.* 2 vols. Paris: Gabalda, 1965.

Stamm, J. J., and Andrew, M. E. *The Ten Commandments in Recent Research.* Naperville, Ill.: Alec R. Allenson, 1967.

Strecker, G. *Handlungsorientierter Glaube: Vorstudien zu einer Ethik des Neuen Testaments.* Stuttgart: Kreuz, 1972.

Weidinger, K. *Die Haufstafeln: Ein Stück urchristlicher Paränese.* Leipzig: Hinrichs, 1928.

Wendland, H. D. *Ethik des Neuen Testaments.* Göttingen: Vandenhoeck & Ruprecht, 1970.

Westerholm, S. *Jesus and Scribal Authority.* Lund: C. W. K. Gleerup, 1978.

Wibbing, S. *Die Tugend- und Lasterkataloge im Neuen Testament und ihre Traditionsgeschichte unter besonderer Berücksichtigung der Qumrantexte.* Berlin: Töpelmann, 1959.

Wilder, A. N. *Eschatology and Ethics in the Teaching of Jesus.* New York: Harper & Brothers, Publishers, 1950.

THE *agapē* MOTIF

Berger, K. *Die Gesetzesauslegung Jesu: Ihr historischer Hintergrund im Judentum und Alten Testament.* Vol. 1. Neukirchen-Vluyn: Neukirchener Verlag, 1972- .

Furnish, V. P. *The Love Command in the New Testament.* Nashville & New York: Abingdon Press, 1972.

Gerhardsson, Birger. *"Hör, Israel!" Om Jesus och den gamla bekännelsen.* Lund: LiberLäromedel, 1979.

Nissen, A. *Gott und der Nächste im antiken Judentum: Untersuchungen zum Doppelgebot der Liebe.* Tübingen: Mohr, 1974.

Nygren, A. *Agape and Eros: A Study of the Christian Idea of Love.* Philadelphia: Westminster Press, 1953; New York: Harper & Row, Publishers, 1969. (Swedish original: *Den kristna kärlekstanken genom tiderna: Eros och agape.* Vols. 1–2. Stockholm: SKDB, 1930–36.)

Outka, G. *Agape: An Ethical Analysis.* (A brilliant analysis of the debate since Nygren.) New Haven and London: Yale University Press, 1972.

Spicq, C. *Agape in the New Testament.* St. Louis: B. Herder Book Co., 1963.

Warnach, V. *Agape: Die Liebe als Grundmotiv der neutestamentlichen Theologie.* Düsseldorf: Patmos, 1951.

DISCIPLESHIP

Betz, H.-D. *Nachfolge und Nachahmung Jesu Christi im Neuen Testament.* Tübingen: Mohr, 1967.

Hengel, M. *Nachfolge und Charisma: Eine exegetisch-religionsgeschichtliche Studie zu Mt 8:21 f und Jesu Ruf in die Nachfolge.* Berlin: Töpelmann, 1968.

Larsson, E. *Christus als Vorbild: Eine Untersuchung zu den paulinischen Tauf- und Eikontexten.* Uppsala and Lund: C. W. K. Gleerup, 1962.

Schulz, A. *Nachfolgen und Nachahmen: Studien über das Verhältnis der neutestamentlichen Jüngerschaft zur urchristlichen Vorbildethik.* Munich: Kösel, 1962.

Biblical References

149